Selections from
'BENGALIANA'

Shoshee Chunder Dutt

Selections from
'BENGALIANA'

Edited by Alex Tickell

TRENT EDITIONS

Published by Trent Editions, 2005

Trent Editions
School of Arts, Communication and Culture
Nottingham Trent University
Clifton Lane
Nottingham NG11 8NS

http://human.ntu.ac.uk/research/trenteditions/mission.html

© This edition: Trent Editions 2005
© Introduction: Alex Tickell 2005

Typeset by Roger Booth Associates, Hassocks, West Sussex BN6 8AR
Printed by Antony Rowe Limited, Bumper's Farm Industrial Estate,
Chippenham, Wiltshire SN14 6LH

ISBN 1-84233-049-7

Contents

Acknowledgements

A number of people have helped me with this project. I would like, firstly, to thank Stephen Minta for arranging a York University travel grant that enabled me to carry out research in India. I also want to thank Elleke Boehmer for her enthusiasm and editorial advice. In the early stages of research Meenakshi Mukherjee and Shubhendu Kumar Mund were both valuable sources of information about Kylas Chunder Dutt. Special thanks go to Amina Yaqin and Peter Morey for discussion and careful assistance with some of the Hindi/Urdu terms in the text. I am also exceptionally grateful to Md. Mahmudul Hasan, who painstakingly looked up many of the *Bangla* words in the glossary. Yet again, I am indebted to Bodh Prakash and Sucheta Mahajan and family for their hospitality, friendship, and help with research on *Bengaliana* in India. In both Delhi and Calcutta, members of the Dutt family were very generous with their assistance, and I would like to thank Malavika Karlekar and Kalyan Dutt in particular. In Calcutta the staff of the National Library were a great help and allowed me access to a number of rare editions of Shoshee's work. Finally, I would like to thank Rachel Goodyear for her advice, support and her invaluable editorial role in the preparation of this edition.

Introduction

Born in 1824 into the highly literary Dutt family and educated at Calcutta's newly established Hindu College, Shoshee (Sasi) Chunder Dutt is one of the most articulate representatives of a new cross-fertilization of European and Bengali culture in early nineteenth-century Calcutta. Remembered chiefly for his religious verse work *A Vision of Sumeru* (1878), which was written after his conversion to Christianity, Shoshee (I will use the *Bangla* convention of referring to the author by his first name) produced ten works in English, several of which were published dually in London and Calcutta. The first member of his family to publish verse in English (in 1848), he was also a prolific prose writer, and the range of his work, which includes historical studies, anthropology, a novel in three volumes, and even crime reportage, reflects the curiosity and intellectual stamina of a nineteenth-century polymath.

The Dutt family were respectable members of Calcutta's Hindu middle class and Shoshee's uncle, Rasamoy Dutt, had made his fortune as a financial consultant for a British firm. This may be why Shoshee was thwarted in his youthful aspirations to become a teacher or literary editor and was, instead, encouraged to take up a comparatively lowly position as an apprentice accounts clerk, or *kerani*, after he graduated from the Hindu College. Shortly afterwards he took a job in the colonial government treasury where his diligence earned him quick promotion; at the same time he started to become known for his journalism. Shoshee Dutt spent most of his subsequent career as Head Assistant at the Bengal Secretariat and was awarded the title of *Rai Bahadur*, or deputy magistrate, in recognition of his thirty-four years of service. He died in 1886. Although he never married, Shoshee had two sons, Suresh and Raman, and also acted as guardian to his orphaned nephews, one of whom, Romesh Chunder Dutt, would later distinguish himself as a brilliant nationalist historian and economist. Shoshee's other nephew, Jogesh Chunder Dutt, recalls the literary influence of his uncle's guardianship thus:

> On the death of our father, our uncle Bubu Shoshee Chunder Dutt came to live in our house in order to bring us up. He too used to sit at night with us and our favourite study used to be pieces from the works of the English poets. Two very important lessons my brother learnt from our uncle—independence of character and thirst for literary fame.[1]

Although largely forgotten today, Shoshee's writing can be located historically at the beginning of what is now known as the Bengal Renaissance, an intellectual and artistic rebirth that started in Calcutta in the early 1800s and reached maturity in the late nineteenth century in the work of writers such as Bankim Chandra Chatterjee and Rabindranath Tagore. However, unlike the later writers of the Bengal Renaissance, who explored and re-examined aspects of indigenous art and literature as part of a burgeoning regional nationalism, Shoshee's work, and the work of his cousins, is marked by a comparative lack of interest in *Bangla* as a literary medium. Indeed, Shoshee's seemingly unambiguous poetic investment in the culture of the colonizer has meant that his prose, while representing some of the earliest fiction in English by a South Asian, has received scant attention in nationalist, Marxist and postcolonial literary histories. The short fictions and journalism selected here from Shoshee's prose collection *Bengaliana* (1877) are significant precisely because they throw into sharp relief the limitations of interpretative strategies that look for signs of agency in emergent cultural nationalisms, subaltern resistance, or in forms of psychic disturbance within the colonial text. Instead, bridging colonial and metropolitan culture, Shoshee's prose is densely inter-discursive and at times derivative, but in its critical edge, humour, and self-confidence it also serves very clearly as the foundation for later, more highly theorized nationalist writing. In *Bengaliana* we encounter a text that satirizes colonial attitudes, imagines armed rebellion against the British, and includes a historical fiction set during the 1857 Mutiny—in short, writing that makes us rethink the scope and sophistication of an elite Indian-English literary response to colonialism in the mid-nineteenth century.

'A Nest of Singing Birds': The Rambagan Dutts

The Dutt family, like the more famous Tagores, made a collective contribution to the intellectual and cultural life of Bengal in the nineteenth century. Originally from the Burdwan district, the family was well-known in Calcutta from the end of the eighteenth century, and its head, Nilmoni Dutt, who set up home in the suburb of Rambagan, was a wealthy and distinguished local figure. Nilmoni's eldest son, Rasamoy Dutt, who was born in 1779, was also prominent in civic life, holding important governing positions in two of Calcutta's new colleges, the Hindu College and the Sanskrit College, as well as acting as a magistrate in the East India Company's small claims court. However, it was not until the succeeding generation and the publication of an extensive corpus of writing by Rasamoy's children and the sons of his younger brother, Pitambur, that the family's literary reputation was established. Rasamoy's sons (Shoshee's cousins) wrote verse, his nephew Romesh Chunder Dutt produced historical novels, translations and economic studies, and his cousin once removed became famous as the poetic child prodigy Toru Dutt.

Rasamoy's second son, Kylas Chunder Dutt, was educated, like his brothers, in the Hindu College that had been founded in 1817, the year of his birth. The College's curricular focus on English and the classics enabled talented young men such as Kylas to test their literary ambitions in the language of the colonizer. While still a student, Kylas published several articles and prose fictions, among which is a remarkable short-story, 'A Journal of Forty-Eight Hours of the Year 1945', published in *The Calcutta Literary Gazette* (6 June 1835), that envisages a popular uprising against British Rule over a century in the future. Kylas was regarded as one of the most gifted students to pass through the Hindu College and, with a student-friend, edited a short-lived monthly journal of his own, *The Hindu Pioneer*. He was awarded first prize at the college for three successive years and after finishing his education rose quickly in the East India Company, becoming a deputy collector in the revenue department while still in his twenties.

Kylas's brothers, Govin (Govind), Hur (Hara), and Greece (Girish), all attended the Hindu College and shared their brother's literary ambitions. Encouraged by the College's principal, David Lester Richardson, who patronized them with the collective title 'the Rambagan nest of singing birds',[2] they produced essays and verse in English and eventually published, with Kylas's son Omesh (Umesh), a collection of their poetry entitled the *Dutt Family Album* in 1870. Some of the contributors to the *Dutt Family Album* were already published poets in their own right, and Hur Chunder Dutt had two collections, *Fugitive Pieces* (1851) and *Lotus Leaves: Poems Chiefly on Ancient Indian Subjects* (1871), to his credit. Greece Chunder Dutt also published a number of volumes of poetry including *The Loyal Hours* (1876), which commemorates visits to India by the Prince of Wales and the Duke of Edinburgh, *Cherry Stones* (1881), and *Cherry Blossoms* (1887). After Rasamoy's death in 1854 his sons converted to Christianity, and from this time onwards their poetry, including much of the verse in the *The Dutt Family Album*, incorporates religious motifs and distinctly Christian themes, sometimes in direct, negative contrast to their representation of Hinduism.

Shoshee Chunder Dutt did not contribute to his cousins' *Family Album*, but he was already publishing essays and short fictions in Calcutta literary journals while still a student of the Hindu College in the mid-1840s. One of his most significant early works is the historical fiction 'The Republic of Orissá: a Page from the Annals of the Twentieth Century', which appeared in

a Calcutta newspaper, *The Saturday Evening Harakura* (25 May 1845). Like
Kylas Chunder Dutt's 'A Journal of Forty-Eight Hours of the Year 1945', this
piece of juvenilia is remarkable for its political prescience (both young men
imagine mass uprisings against British in the twentieth century) and its
daring appropriation of a late-romantic European vocabulary of political
rights. Because both stories display such strong formal and thematic
similarities, Kylas Chunder Dutt's 'A Journal of Forty-Eight Hours of the Year
1945' has been included in a coda to this selection of Shoshee Chunder
Dutt's writing.

THE HINDU COLLEGE AND YOUNG BENGAL

Throughout his writing Shoshee emphasizes the formative nature of his
education at the Hindu College, and goes as far as to describe one of the
college founders, the Scottish educationalist David Hare, as an almost
mythical philanthropic figure 'to this day venerated as one of the *griha-
devatás* or household gods of Calcutta'.[3] With the orientalist scholar H. H.
Wilson and David Hyde East, the Chief Justice of the Calcutta Supreme
Court, Hare had set up a committee in 1816 for the establishment of an
institution that would teach a European-style curriculum, and the Hindu
College was inaugurated the following year. From its inception, the project
was also supported by the great educationalist, reformer, and organizer of the
Brahmo Sabha, Rammohan Roy. Thus, with a mixed governing body that
included important Bengali citizens such as Rammohan and Shoshee's uncle
Rasamoy Dutt, the scheme responded to a widespread interest in European-
style learning, and reveals how involved Calcutta's indigenous elites were in
debates over their own education at the time. Because of this cross-cultural
involvement, the Hindu College should not be seen, in retrospect, as an
institutional conduit for European assimilation (although it inevitably took
on this role under Lord Bentinck's governor-generalship) but as a product of
the broader reforms and changes that shaped Indian society as part of the
colonial encounter. Indeed, the middle-class Indians who campaigned for the
college actually pre-empted colonial policy, which did not officially formalize
tuition in English until almost two decades later, when Thomas Babington
Macaulay called for a new interpreter class of indigenous English-speakers in
his famous 'Minute on Education' of 1835.[4]

It is apt that the most famous representative of this new, intrinsically
hybrid educational institution was, himself, of mixed race. The flamboyant
poet Henry Louis Vivian Derozio, who was of Portuguese and Indian
parentage, was employed as a teacher at the Hindu College between 1826 and
1831, and his radical political ideas and intellectual charisma influenced a

generation of students. Although he was only seventeen when he joined the college, Derozio could already critique Kantian philosophy and in 1828 published a collection of romantic lyric poems, including 'The Harp of India' in which he lamented India's colonial subjection. It has been claimed that Derozio's poetry represents a nascent Indian nationalism, although David Kopf offers a more guarded interpretation when he locates Derozio's politics in terms of his 'faith in the eighteenth century ideal of universality' and his 'Byronic sense of style'.[5] Derozio proved to be an inspired teacher, and his students, known collectively as 'Young Bengal', became notorious for their progressivism. Encouraged by Derozio, they read revolutionary thinkers such as Thomas Paine, 'ridiculed old traditions, defied ... social and religious rites, demanded education for women', and, most scandalously of all, 'indulged in wine-drinking and beef-eating'.[6] Derozio was eventually dismissed from the college for allegedly corrupting its students, but even after his premature death in 1831 his influence persisted in the political debating societies and lobby-groups set up by his former pupils.

It is unlikely that Kylas or Shoshee Chunder Dutt would have come into direct contact with Derozio, but in the 1830s and '40s the intellectual environment of the Hindu College was still marked by a Eurocentric Derozian progressivism, and both the classical interests and the political radicalism of Young Bengal inform the Dutts' early writing (especially works such as Shoshee's 'The Republic of Orissá' and Kylas's 'A Journal of Forty Eight-Hours'). However, in Shoshee's prose it is the English principal of the Hindu College, the poet and editor David Lester Richardson, rather than Derozio, who is mentioned as a mentor and influence. In his most autobiographical work, 'Reminiscences of a Kerání's Life', Dutt's middle-aged narrator wryly recalls himself with 'a noodle's head full of bombast and fustian ... raw from school, with the melodious warblings of D. L. R. still rumbling in [my] brains'. As college principal, Richardson responded conservatively to the more libertarian opinions of Young Bengal, which he thought verged on the seditious, but he also acknowledged Derozio's posthumous literary and intellectual influence and encouraged his students' literary efforts. As well as providing 'melodious' rhetorical inspiration, Richardson published a number of pieces of work by his students (including 'A Journal of Forty-Eight Hours') in his journal, *The Calcutta Literary Gazette.*

SHOSHEE CHUNDER DUTT: PUBLISHED WORKS
Shoshee Chunder Dutt's poetry and prose had featured regularly in newspapers and journals in Calcutta before his first edition of poems entitled

Miscellaneous Verses appeared in 1848. The first major publication in English by any member of the Dutt family, Shoshee's *Miscellaneous Verses* comprises poems that draw thematically on Indian legends and episodes in medieval history, and was later expanded and reprinted as *A Vision of Sumeru and Other Poems* (1878). In this later edition the title poem, 'A Vision of Sumeru', which recounts the symbolic overthrow of the gods of the Hindu pantheon by the morally superior teachings of the Bible, echoes the evangelical tenor of some poems in the *Dutt Family Album*. Its exotic cultural references and heavy annotation also recall contemporary English orientalist poetry.[7] However, Shoshee was as much an essayist, historian, and ethnologist as a poet. Only a few years after *Miscellaneous Verses* he published a selection of his journalism entitled *Essays on Miscellaneous Subjects* (1854). These essays anticipate his later interests and include political reflections on his own generation ('Young Bengal; or the Hopes of India'), tracts on religious and social reform movements ('Vedantism and Brumha Subha' and 'Hindu Female Education'), and essays that appropriate the distinctive tone of colonial ethnography ('The Rohilla Afghans'). The essays reappeared, some in revised form, in a later work entitled *Stray Leaves; or Essays, Poems and Tables*, published in Calcutta in 1864, in which Shoshee develops his role as a largely pro-colonial legislator for 'native' Bengal, and provides commentaries on the 'Training of Native Youths in Europe' and tracts on Hindu caste and mythology.

The surviving editions of Shoshee's work from the late 1870s bear the imprints of London publishers, a change noted by Rosinka Chaudhuri in her study of nineteenth-century poetry in Bengal, where she points out that by this time London 'had become the primary choice for any poet writing in English … as publications from India were no longer assured the attention accorded them in the earlier days of East India Company rule'.[8] Because of this shift the Dutts effectively became 'the first Indian writers to be published, sometimes simultaneously, in both India and England'[9] and a new awareness of their expanded trans-cultural readership explains, to some extent, the more celebratory, pro-colonial statements and orientalist borrowings in their writing. Significantly, Shoshee also starts using English pseudonyms at this stage in his career (possibly at the insistence of his publishers), and relies increasingly on the discursive authority of academic genres such as the historical textbook or the ethnographic 'manners and customs' account.

The first of Shoshee's pseudonymous works is his two-volume *Historical Studies and Recreations* (1879), which was originally published under the name J. A. G. Barton, a *nom de plume* he seems to have favoured for histories because he uses it again in his chronicle of Bengal in 1884, and in *The Great Wars of India* published in the same year. In contrast, his rambling three volume *bildungsroman*, *The Young Zaminadar* (1883), as well as an ethnological study *The Wild Tribes of India* (1882), were written under another, more outlandish pseudonym: Horatio Bickerstaffe Rowney. In the latter work, his interest in India's *adivasi* (tribal) communities and his careful classification of different ethnic groupings are impressive examples of a covert appropriation of pseudo-scientific colonial descriptive modes. Alongside the ethnographic monograph we also find Shoshee employing another of the stock descriptive modes of colonial writing, often combined with 'manners and customs' accounts: the area-study. In *Bengal, An Account of the Country from the Earliest Times* (1884) his focus includes Bengal's economic history, its 'antiquarian relics', and characteristically the 'classification of the people'. Anticipating the work of colonial ethnographers such as Herbert H. Risley, Shoshee colludes with emergent imperialist ideas about racial difference in this text, reproducing a form of racial pathetic fallacy in his differentiation of ethnic types in Bengal, where 'people inhabiting the mountainous and infertile regions are hardy and laborious [sic] while those inhabiting the moist climates, with their double crops of rice and infinite variety of pulses are indolent and effeminate'.[10]

The objective, positivist tone of studies such as *The Wild Tribes of India*, combined with the mask of an English pseudonym, make it difficult to evaluate exactly how Shoshee relates to his subject matter in these works, but some of his comments suggest that his representation of 'tribal' groups may have involved a significant displacement of personal political frustration. Shoshee had chosen an *adivasi* clan, the *Kingáries*, as the basis of his fantasy of anti-colonial conflict in 'The Republic of Orissá', and later, during the 1880s, a growing sense of Bengali nationalist pride would be articulated through the example of the 'tribal' uprisings against the British. Along with recovered legends of Rajput valour, culturally unassimilated insurgent tribal communities provided an urban literati with potent symbols of independence, and sharp reminders of their own deracination. Colonial accounts of tribal rebellions form the basis of important nationalist fictions in *Bangla* such as Bankim Chandra Chatterjee's *Anandamath* (1882),[11] and Shoshee's 'tribal' studies, although masquerading as ethnography, cannot wholly avoid these more political inferences. In *The Wild Tribes* his presentation of Indian 'savagery' wavers between disdain and admiration when he states that the 'one redeeming feature' of subaltern *adivasi* groups is 'their utter abhorrence of thraldom and despotism'.[12]

The use of a quasi-anthropological narrative style continues in another of Shoshee Dutt's works, *Realities of Indian Life* (1885), which is subtitled '*Stories Collated from the Criminal Reports of India to Illustrate the Life, Manners, and*

Customs of its Inhabitants. Here, the claim to the authority of the 'manners and customs' account lends moral weight to a series of sensational crime stories, some of which revisit the two primary *loci* of colonial reform in the early nineteenth century: *sati*, or widow-immolation, and *thugs*, criminal sects who sacrificed their victims to the goddess *Kali*. In 'collating' his stories, Shoshee may have drawn on his experiences as a deputy magistrate, and these reports show us again how attuned he was to the reception of his work overseas. In the mid-1880s various spiritualist and occult groups such as Madame Blavatsky's Theosophy movement popularized Yoga and forms of Vedic mysticism in Britain and the United States, and Dutt's stories, with titles such as 'The Spirit Voice', 'The Sister-Sutee', and 'The Irresolute Suttee', would have pandered to this metropolitan interest. *Realities of Indian Life* is also noteworthy because it represents an early version of the Indian detective narrative (later developed by Satyajit Ray in his 'Feluda' stories) and demonstrates how the detective genre shared considerable epistemological space with the new nineteenth-century disciplines of ethnology and anthropology.

BENGALIANA

Shoshee Chunder Dutt's *Bengaliana: A dish of Rice and Curry, and Other Indigestible Ingredients,* a collection of journalistic and prose-pieces published by Thacker, Spink and Co. in Calcutta in 1877/8 but printed in London, exemplifies more than any of his other works the range of Shoshee Dutt's interests, and includes semi-autobiographical writing alongside historical essays, fiction, and fragments of documentary reportage. In critical assessments of Dutt's work, *Bengaliana* has often been classed as a minor, ephemeral work, the prose marginalia of a writer who was more interested in poetry. This emphasis on Shoshee's poetic career is unfortunate since his verse often reads as a cumbersome, technically unsophisticated tribute to the English romantics.[13] Conversely, many of the prose pieces that appear in *Bengaliana* were never originally intended for the same (potentially international) readership as the poems, and are both more complex and politically more revealing than his verse.

The fact that these are writings that developed out of the polyglot world of the early nineteenth-century colonial contact zone is evidenced in the title of Shoshee's collection. *Bengaliana* is a bilingual pun, and can be defined broadly as 'Bengali-ness' in *Bangla*, as well as having more classical generic connotations in English.[14] The collection's intriguing subtitle points up the potential strangeness of the text for readers unfamiliar with India (presenting it as a buffet of dangerous literary exotica unsuited to metropolitan taste), but also locates the work firmly within the traditions of English literature, with an epigraph from the eighteenth-century actor and dramatist David Garrick attesting to the 'unadulterated' truth of the work. Shoshee's stylistic debt to eighteenth-century prose is also apparent in the culinary metaphor of the title, reminiscent of Henry Fielding's famous 'bill of fare' passage at the beginning of *Tom Jones*, in which the contents of the novel are described as a series of mixed dishes comprising human nature. These prose pieces are also culturally anchored in the work of orientalists such as William Jones, but also (in pieces such as 'Reminiscences of a Keráni's Life') the classical, Latinate allusions and developing modes of political and cultural satire of eighteenth-century prose.

Today, the appeal of these works lies in their discursive energy and verbal inventiveness, and the fact that they seem to escape the more contrived orientalist techniques of nineteenth-century Indian poetry in English. Because of the informal intimacy of the journalistic mode, the voices resounding through these works have a distinctive idiomatic ring, as Shoshee exploits a developing Anglo-Indian argot consisting of a mish-mash of nouns, adjectives, and hybrid neologisms boiled down from *Hindustani* and *Bangla*, seasoning an ornate, sometimes bookish English—a portmanteau language that would eventually be standardized in dictionaries such as *Hobson-Jobson*. The dialogic quality of Shoshee's writing is readily apparent in 'The Street Music of Calcutta', in which the cries of street-vendors passing the narrator's house are all meticulously transcribed, presenting us with a fascinating sound-picture of contemporary Calcutta, with its brandy-bottle collectors, beggars, and *dal* sellers. Compared with the heavily embroidered Orient of later, more stylized 'street-music' poems such as Sarojini Naidu's 'Songs of my City', which take the reader through an Aladdin's cave of brocade tunics and jade-handled daggers[15] Shoshee's 'street music' has a compelling, auditory realism.

If some of Shoshee's prose pieces such as 'The Republic of Orissá' look forward historically to the twentieth century, the digressive, linguistic inventiveness of his writing anticipates the formal experimentations of postcolonial fictions such as G.V. Desani's dizzying, idiosyncratic work *All About H. Hatterr* (1948) or 'mongrel' fictions such as Salman Rushdie's *Midnight's Children* (1981). But unlike its postcolonial descendents, the politics of *Bengaliana* are far from unified, and the collection reminds us of the continual trans-cultural negotiations and split allegiances of Bengal's colonially-educated native elite. This said, *Bengaliana,* unlike the more patriotic sections of Shoshee's *A Vision of Sumeru* or his defence of the *Pax Britannica* in *Bengal,* is more ambivalent and more covertly critical of aspects of colonial rule than we might expect, especially from an author whose decision to continue writing in English well into the 1870s countered the prevailing nationalist bias towards *Bangla* literature. Leaving aside the early political fantasy 'The Republic of Orissá', the sense of agency in Shoshee's work is mediated, for the most part, through irony and anecdotal understatement, a strategy that relies on an intimate, sometimes weary knowledge of the colonial information-order.

Shoshee's 'Reminiscences of a Keráni's Life' provides the most pertinent example of this critical insiderism, and reminds us, again, of the priorities of colonial discourse analysis as an interpretative mode concerned more with absences and shadows in colonial writing, and with what the colonial text *doesn't* say, than the actual conflicts, strategic manoeuvres and double-edged exchanges apparent in writing by the colonized. Intriguingly, Shoshee's 'Reminiscences' takes us to the heart of the East India Company, the great accounting machine of the colonial treasury, regulated by an intricate print-culture of bills and counter receipts. With its rivalries, one-upmanship and shifting loyalties this is, however, also a quintessentially modern setting, that of the office, a place where 'a very great amount of forbearance and philosophy is necessary to override the petty evils of life'. It is in this environment that we become aware of the political leverage available to Anglicized Indians because of a colonial institutional dependency on transcultural interpreters, a form of agency that operates as a clandestine, ambivalent strategy of personal advancement within the institution. With a shrewd awareness of bureaucratic power, Shoshee's text tallies its accounts ledger of personal triumphs: the arrogant *memsahib* who is refused preferential treatment because of the strictness of banking times; the incompetent European sub-manager who is saved by the narrator's Jeeves-like ability to anticipate (and circumvent) his blunders; and the numerous smaller victories that add up to something approaching self-determination in the face of colonial racism.

In 'Reminiscences' Shoshee also reflects on wider historical issues, in particular the anti-colonial rebellion or Mutiny which swept across north India (but did not seriously affect Calcutta) in 1857. Commenting on the counter-insurgent silencing of Indian versions of the Mutiny, the narrator of the 'Reminiscences' claims that he risks being 'set down as a mutineer myself if I attempted [to write about] it', and suggests ironically that 'we must leave it to Englishmen to tell the story for us ... I have no doubt that, sooner or later, the tale will be most faithfully told'. The double-edged implication that a 'true' version of the Mutiny has yet to be written emphasizes the hegemonic uniformity of the colonial novels and accounts that proliferated after the conflict. It also throws into perspective the relative novelty of another text reprinted in *Bengaliana*, a historical-fiction that clearly attempts to do exactly what the narrator of the 'Reminiscences' disavows: to tell the story of the Mutiny from the perspective of the colonized.

Shoshee's 'Shunkur: A Tale of the Indian Mutiny', written in 1877, is unique because it is an Indian-English fiction that engages not only with the Mutiny, but with one of its most notorious episodes: the massacre of European women and children in Cawnpore [Kanpur] by the rebel leader, Nana Saheb. In her feminist study of colonial writing, Jenny Sharpe has argued that colonial accounts of the Cawnpore incident fulfil a complex discursive function, managing the crisis of colonial authority during the Mutiny by challenging the truth value of native 'rumour', and refiguring rebellion in the trope of the raped or mutilated European woman. In fact, these narratives stage women as little more than bodies to be violated (and avenged), effacing, in Sharpe's opinion, the more disturbing prospect of the loss of male political control: 'From the perspective of the colonizer, once a European man is struck down, then anything is possible; in death his mortality is exposed and sovereign status is brought low'.[16] As Sharpe argues, 'A discourse of rape—that is the violent reproduction of gender roles—helped manage the crisis in authority so crucial to colonial self representation at the time'.[17]

In 'Shunkur', Shoshee's reference to the highly emotive Cawnpore massacre can be read as a perilous engagement with the meta-narratives of colonial counter-insurgency. Indeed, in a passing reference to Shoshee's writing, Jnanendra Nath Gupta claims that on publication the story 'startled Sir Erskine Perry and Sir Ashley Eden by its strange disclosures, and there was some correspondence with the government on the subject'.[18] Because of the sensitivity of his material, Shoshee does not provide a corrective to the stock colonial representation of Nana Saheb (as a villainous bluebeard-figure) but instead nuances the political origins of rebellion, presenting them as part of a Russian plot against British supremacy in India. Elsewhere, anti-colonial insurgency is portrayed not as a political objective but as an inevitable symptom of colonial misrule. Building on these attempts to finesse a historical understanding of the motives of the rebels, Shoshee risks a more radical reversal of the conventions of colonial discourse in his treatment of the abiding rape metaphor discussed earlier. While relating Nana Saheb's 'treacherous and cowardly' disloyalty, and echoing the hagiographic style of colonial descriptions of the massacre—'Poor brave English hearts! ... in what page of history shall we read an account to equal your heroic sufferings?'— 'Shunkur' also follows the fortunes of two European fugitives from Cawnpore, Bernard and Mackenzie, who are hidden from the rebel soldiers by an Indian woman and her daughter. In a chapter grimly entitled 'The Requital', these European fugitives repay the hospitality of their protectors by

raping the daughter before they leave, a reworking of the trope of violated
womanhood that responds symbolically to Nana Saheb's (sexualized)
mutilation of European woman.

Attempts like this to 'balance' the politics of the Mutiny-account inform
Shoshee's revenge-plot, in which the gradual restoration of colonial authority
by the relief forces of General Neill and General Havelock is matched by the
quest for personal justice embarked upon by the main protagonist, Shunkur
(who turns out to be the husband of the Indian woman raped by Bernard and
Mackenzie). This doubled structure allows Shoshee to contrast the
notoriously brutal and arbitrary reprisals of military leaders such as Neill with
the more personal sense of injury felt by Shunkur. In an aside that satirizes
the 'heroic' zeal of British military justice, we are told that on hearing of the
arrest of a Mahomedan, a 'Hindu of substance', and a *sepoy*, or soldier, Neill's
commanding officer orders them all to be hanged from the nearest tree
because 'The Mahomedan must be a traitor; the Hindu, since he has
substance, must have acquired it unfairly; and the sepoy is necessarily a
mutineer'. However, this quietly satirical reference to the arbitrary violence of
British reprisals never develops into an interrogation of the legitimacy of
colonial rule. Nor does 'Shunkur' challenge the characteristic colonial troping
of rebellion in terms of rape; it simply offers us a counter-narrative involving
the rape of an equally passive and emblematic Indian woman. Yet for all its
rhetorical circumspection and formal clumsiness (the narrative ends abruptly
as if its serialization was terminated hastily), 'Shunkur' represents an unusual
and comparatively daring attempt to counter the political and historical
truth-claims of colonial writing on the Mutiny.

IMAGINING REBELLION

It is clear, then, that Shoshee and contemporaries such as Kylas Chunder
Dutt exploited a margin of allowable dissent in their writings in English. In
Bengaliana, Shoshee also appropriates various dialogic and reiterative
techniques from English prose traditions in order to reflect the more
oppressive points of British rule back to his colonial readers. But in the
majority of his writings this critical capacity is checked by a cultural and
religious investment in colonial society. As Sudhir Chandra states, 'faith in
colonialism despite and understanding of its exploitativeness—this was the
paradox of educated consciousness in colonial India'.[19] And the more we read
of Shoshee's work, the more this 'paradoxical' balancing act explains the
internal tensions in specific texts, and underlies the different critical tenor of
his poetry and prose, especially where these operate across the new diverging
reader-communities of metropolitan centre and colonial periphery. This said,

two early short stories already mentioned in this introduction—Kylas Chunder Dutt's 'A Journal of Forty-Eight Hours of the Year 1945' and Shoshee Chunder Dutt's 'The Republic of Orissá: A Page from the Annals of the Twentieth Century'—are outstanding in their uncompromising critical treatment of British rule in India, and in their futuristic visions of anti-colonial liberation.

As well as having a reasonable claim to be the 'earliest extant narrative [English] texts in India',[20] these two short fictions are also works by students—Kylas was only eighteen when his story was published. It is perhaps because of their obvious status as juvenilia, and the comparatively indulgent attitude of the colonial authorities towards publications of this kind in the 1830s and '40s, that these prophetic rebellion-narratives, both of which draw on the radical tradition of Derozio and Young Bengal, were published at all. (It is certainly difficult to envisage their publication after 1857.) In both cases, the use of a futuristic historical setting produces a caricatured, chronologically distanced picture of British rule, while at the same time allowing both authors to make provocative associations between their own lack of political freedom and contemporary issues such as the debate over slavery and Jacobin radicalism.

The intellectual imprimatur of Young India is clearest in Kylas's 'Journal of Forty-Eight Hours', a story about an armed anti-colonial rebellion in mid-twentieth century Calcutta, fomented by fifty years of 'subaltern oppression and … deep and dreadful provocation'. The rebellion is led by the distinctly Derozian hero, Bhoobun Mohun, 'splendidly attired in kincaub and gold', who addresses his followers with all the 'learning and eloquence which the Anglo-Indian college could furnish'. After a stirringly patriotic speech, Kylas's student-protagonist leads his countrymen into a skirmish with the British troops sent to disperse them. The rebels win an early victory, and attack Fort William the next day, but their cause is betrayed by the treachery of the British viceroy, 'Lord Fell Butcher', and by a lack of indigenous support, and Bhoobun Mohan is captured and executed. With historical hindsight, some details of Kylas's story are unerring: his rebel heroes style themselves the 'supreme power [in India] … the leaders of the national convention', and their fight for independence occurs in 1945, just two years before the Indian National Congress would actually win India's freedom. However, it would be unrealistic to expect the narrative to provide a comprehensive or structured account of a proto-national uprising against the British. Instead the story is an engaging series of set-piece speeches and 'gladiatorial' combats that bear testimony to its colonial literary influences. At the start of his narrative Kylas seems poised to enter into a direct dialogue with his literary antecedents (in this case perhaps Edmund Burke's anti-revolutionary study *Reflections on the Revolution in France*) when he states 'It is easy for the historian and the bard to depict in most lively colours the excesses committed by revolutionary parties, but he only can truly judge who has been a fellow sufferer [of oppressive rule]'. Elsewhere, the narrative relies on forms of stylistic quotation, and shades of Mark Anthony's oration in *Julius Caesar* creep into Bhoobun Mohun's 'friends and countrymen' address to the rebels.

Shoshee Chunder Dutt's 'Republic of Orissá', published in the *Saturday Evening Harakura* in May 1845, while employing the same technique of historical projection, envisages anti-colonial rebellion rather differently from its companion piece. Longer and structurally more complex than Kylas's story, and incorporating an embedded romance plot reminiscent of the legend of Prithviraj and Sanjogita, 'The Republic of Orissá' tells the story of an *adivasi* (tribal) uprising against the British after slavery is reimposed in the Indian empire in 1916. Unlike the failed Jacobin coup in Kylas's story, Shoshee's army of tribal Kingaries is victorious, and after a pitched battle outside Delhi the British are forced to concede regional independence to Orissa, which becomes a moral beacon for decolonization: 'a splendid spectacle ... a nation emerging from the chaos of ignorance and slavery, and hastening to occupy its orbit on the grand system of civilization'. As in his other writings, the rebellion narrative allows Shoshee to interrogate colonial moral certainties, and includes an elaborate parody of benevolent utilitarian rhetoric in which an English journalist protests that in India 'slavery, now constituted, hardly approaches the "durance vile" of a common every-day labourer'.

That it is the reintroduction of slavery into India that catalyses rebellion in 'The Republic of Orissá' is likely to have had some historical basis. In 1843 the well-known British abolitionist George Thompson spoke at several meetings in Calcutta organized by Derozio's former students.[21] Thompson was a member of the British India Society, which pushed for labour reforms in India as a way of pricing American plantation-grown cotton and sugar out of the global market. His speech was so well received in India that the short-lived Bengal British India Society was set up on 20 April 1843 with the object of protecting the 'legitimate rights of [India's] subjects'.[22] Shoshee's representation of anti-colonial rebellion as an *adivasi* uprising, while reflecting specific anthropological ideas about a 'tribal' antipathy to political subjugation, also points up the prevalence of actual peasant insurgency in nineteenth-century India. Just two years before the Mutiny of 1857 over thirty thousand Santals rebelled, and it is therefore understandable that India's aboriginal groups should become the most likely instigators of rebellion in Shoshee's pre-Mutiny narrative.

Both these fictions are thinly disguised political allegories, but we can also read them more literally as pragmatic recognition on the part of the colonized of how *long* colonialism would last. In the second of his theses on the philosophy of history, Walter Benjamin draws attention to Lotze's observation that 'One of the most remarkable characteristics of human nature is, alongside so much selfishness in specific instances, the freedom from envy which the present displays toward the future',[23] but perhaps in these fictional projections of liberation-struggle far into the future we *are* presented with a form of envy for the yet-to-come. Certainly, in Shoshee's writing the rebellion in Orissa accompanies a wistful fantasy of imperial decline redolent of Gibbon: 'the British Empire is sinking fast into that state of weakness and internal division which is the sure forerunner of the fall of kingdoms'. It would be a hundred years before British colonialism in India came to an end, and its demise would not be at the hands of tribal warriors but through the organization, campaigning, and brilliant political theorizing of a colonially-educated Indian middle class—intellectuals very like Shoshee himself. Mindful of, but not yet 'weighed down by the burden of servility'[24] which the English language conferred on many of his contemporaries, Shoshee's work foreshadows the confident humanism of this later generation, and forms a compelling prelude to the literature of decolonization.

NOTES

1. Quoted in Rabindra Chandra Dutt, *Romesh Chunder Dutt* (New Delhi: Government Publications Division, 1968), p. 11.
2. See Harihar Das, *The Life and Letters of Toru Dutt* (London: Humphrey Milford, 1921), p. 16.
3. Shoshee Chunder Dutt, *Bengal, An Account of the Country from the Earliest Times* (London: Gilbert and Rivington, 1884), p. 156.
4. Thomas Babington Macaulay, 'Minute on Indian Education' in *Selected Writings: Thomas Babington Macaulay*, ed. John Clive and Thomas Pinney (Chicago: University of Chicago Press, 1972), pp. 237-251.
5. David Kopf, *British Orientalism and the Bengal Renaissance: The Dynamics of Indian Modernisation 1773-1835* (Calcutta: Firma K. L Mukhopadhyay, 1969), p.255.
6. Susobhan Sarkar, *On the Bengal* Renaissance, 3rd edn (Calcutta: Papyrus, 2002), p. 24.
7. Rosinka Chaudhuri, *Gentleman Poets in Colonial Bengal: Emergent Nationalism and the Orientalist Project* (Calcutta: Seagull, 2002), p. 135.
8. Ibid., p. 133.
9. Ibid.
10. Shoshee Chunder Dutt, *Bengal, An Account of the Country from the Earliest Times* (London: Gilbert and Rivington, 1884), p. 117.

11. For a perceptive discussion of Bankim's influences, see Sudipta Kaviraj, *The Unhappy Consciousness: Bankimchandra Chattopadhyay and the Formation of Nationalist Discourse in India* (New Delhi: Oxford University Press, 1995).

12. Horatio Bickerstaffe Rowney, *The Wild Tribes of India* (London: Thomas De la Rue and Co., 1882), p. xv.

13. For a particularly negative assessment of Shoshee's poetry, see Lotika Basu, *Indian Writers of English Verse* (Calcutta: Calcutta University Press, 1933).

14. I am indebted to Professor Kalyan Dutt for this observation about *Bengaliana*.

15. See Sarojini Naidu's verse collection *The Golden Threshold* (London: William Heinemann, 1905). I am indebted to Professor Elleke Boehmer for making the connection between Shoshee and Sarojini Naidu.

16. Jenny Sharpe, *Allegories of Empire: The Figure of Woman in the Colonial Text* (Minneapolis: University of Minnesota Press, 1993), p. 67.

17. Ibid.

18. Jnanendra Nath Gupta, *Life and Work of Romesh Chunder Dutt* (London: J. M. Dent and Sons, 1911), p. 7.

19. Sudhir Chandra, *The Oppressive Present* (New Delhi: Oxford University Press, 1992), p. 46.

20. Meenakshi Mukherjee, *The Perishable Empire: Essays on Indian Writing in English* (New Delhi: Oxford University Press, 2000), p. 52.

21. Susobhan Sarkar, *On the Bengal Renaissance*, 3rd edn (Calcutta: Papyrus, 2002), p. 24.

22. Ibid., p. 26.

23. Walter Benjamin, *Illuminations* ed. Hannah Arendt, trans. Harry Zohn (London: Fontana/Harper Collins, 1992), p. 245.

24. Meenakshi Mukherjee, *The Perishable Empire: Essays on Indian Writing in English* (New Delhi: Oxford University Press, 2000), p. 55.

Suggestions for Further Reading

A brief critical discussion of Shoshee and Kylas Chunder Dutt's early historical writing can be found in Meenakshi Mukherjee's pioneering work on early Indian fiction in English, *The Perishable Empire: Essays on Indian Writing in English* (New Delhi: Oxford University Press, 2000). For a detailed analysis of the Dutt family's poetic work, Rosinka Chaudhuri's monograph *Gentleman Poets in Colonial Bengal: Emergent Nationalism and the Orientalist Project* (Calcutta: Seagull, 2002) is invaluable, as is her chapter on the *Dutt Family Album* in Arvind Krishna Mehrotra's *A History of Indian Literature in English* (London: Hurst, 2003). The latter also includes an informative chapter by Sajni Kripalani Mukherji on The Hindu College and Henry Derozio. Shubhendu Kumar Mund discusses Shoshee's work in *The Indian Novel in English: Its Birth and Development* (New Delhi: Prachi Prakashan, 1997), and another older literary-historical study is John B. Alphonso-Karkala's *Indo-English Literature in the Nineteenth Century* (Mysore: Mysore University Press, 1970). Alphonso-Karkala covers a number of important authors but his references to Shoshee are minimal and sometimes confused. For a highly critical evaluation of Shoshee's poetic writings, see Lotika Basu's interesting (but dated) *Indian Writers of English Verse* (Calcutta: University of Calcutta, 1933).

There is very little biographical material available on Shoshee Chunder Dutt, and I have drawn on Jnanendra Nath Gupta's *Life and Work of Romesh Chunder Dutt* (London: J. M. Dent and Sons, 1911) and Rabindra Chandra Dutt's *Romesh Chunder Dutt* (New Delhi: Government Publications Division, 1968) for details of Shoshee's life. For a thoughtful contextual analysis of the cultural background of *Bengaliana*, see David Kopf's *British Orientalism and the Bengal Renaissance: The Dynamics of Indian Modernisation 1773-1835* (Calcutta: Firma K.L. Mukhopadhyay, 1969). Susobhan Sarkar's *On The Bengal Renaissance* (Papyrus: Calcutta, 2002) is another useful overview of the period, and contains sections on David Hare and Derozio's Young Bengal movement.

A Note on the Text

This edition draws selectively from Shoshee Chunder Dutt's *Bengaliana, A dish of Rice and Curry, and Other Indigestible Ingredients* (Calcutta: Thaker, Spink and Co., 1877/8) and readers should consult the original text for a comprehensive view of its contents. My choices have been dictated by the originality and technical or thematic novelty of the fictional and journalistic pieces included here.

Reminiscences of a Keráni's Life

[By Shoshee Chunder Dutt. From *Bengaliana: A dish of Rice and Curry, and Other Indigestible Ingredients.*]

CHAPTER I. A MERCHANT'S APPRENTICE

Thirty years ago! Well, thirty years is a very long time to look back upon. The old man with grey hair and grey beard now before you had not then yet attained the last of his teens, and was enjoying the full vigour of his youth, with a noodle's head full of bombast and fustian, and a vigorous imagination, building all sorts of castles in the air.

Thirty years ago! What changes have occurred since then, how many friends have dropt off, how many pleasures have been numbered with the dead, how many recollections crowd on the brain and addle it!

Well, I was yet a youngster then; not quite a boy, but hardly yet a man; slim and not ungainly,—I may say so now when I am as ungainly as a human being can be; my youthful memory stocked with quotations from Shakespeare, Milton, and Bacon; regarding myself as a prodigy not unequal to the admirable Crichton.[1]

Raw from school, with the melodious warblings of D.L.R.* still rumbling in his brains, what was this young man to do to commence with? Of course he could start a newspaper or a magazine; nothing, in his estimation, was easier: or, better still, he could write books for the edification of mankind in general, and the Hindu race in particular; or he might become a pedagogue, and for the benefit of others unload his brain of the perilous stuff that was playing the deuce with it. All these appeared to him to be quite easy and feasible, and promised more wealth (a consideration never to be lost sight of) than Alládin's lamp had ever fetched. But papa shook his head, and said 'Nay' to every brilliant idea as it cropped up, and the upshot was that, at the age of eighteen, I joined the respectable firm of Smasher, Mutton, and Co., as an apprentice.

There were no conveyances in those days for apprentices, though now there are. The number of *ticcá ghárries* was very small—scarcely enough to meet the requirements of well-paid keránis; and the number of *ticcá pálkees* was still less. Those, therefore, who drew no pay, did not think it *infra dig.* to

* David Lester Richardson, Principal and Professor of Literature, Hindu College

trudge to office on foot; and if any found the sun too hot for him, there was the *chátá*, a very respectable protection for the head—I mean those *bursátee chátás* with long poles, which—alas! for poetry and romance—have now become extinct.

Well, protected by a *chátá*, and with a high *pugree* on my head (my first attempt to make one without previous study being necessarily very clumsy), I appeared before Mr. Pigeon, the managing clerk of the firm of Smasher, Mutton, and Co., and made as stiff a *salaám* as any Young Bengal has rendered either before or after that era. Mr. Pigeon received the obeisance with a smile. Of course he did not return it; no one has ever returned the *salaám* of an apprentice. 'What did I know? What would I wish to learn? Did I understand accounts? Did I know what a ledger was? Could I docket a letter, or draft a reply?'—these and many other equally impertinent questions were launched out with mortifying volubility. They were all Greek to me; I had learnt English, but no Greek; I had never come across such uncouth words as 'ledger,' 'docket,' or 'draft!'

With smiling hopelessness Mr. Pigeon made me over to his head Báboo, Kinoorám Chuckerbutty, to make of me what he could; and with supercilious contempt the Báboo told me to mend his pens. Was Young Bengal to submit to this? Shades of Bacon, Addison, and Johnson,[2] was the student who had kept company with you so long, and pored over your pages night and morning, now to mend the pens of an old *keráni*? But then, another thought also arose. Was the very first day of apprenticeship to be signalized by a revolt? My young noddle was troubled and vexed; the pens were mended in moody silence and discontent.

I had no idea before that I understood *duftry's* work so well. Kinoo Báboo could not mend pens himself, and those mended by me were to his liking. He became very gracious, gave me small additions and subtractions to work out—*e. g.* coolie-hire so much, add to it punka-puller's wages, then deduct floating-balances in hand, &c.; and I soon came to the conclusion that I kept the entire accounts of the firm though Kinoorám drew the pay. The very important duty of entering letters in the peon's book came also to be assigned to me; and by the end of a fortnight I thought I had fairly established a claim to a salary of at least a hundred rupees to commence with.

The fortnight past, I made a low *salaám* to Mr. Pigeon; not so stiff as on the first occasion, and yet sufficiently so to indicate that I was of the Young Bengal genus, which Kinoorám was not; and I asked how Mr. Pigeon thought I was working. There was the same smile as before, but the words were not encouraging.

'I have seen no work from you yet. What have you been doing?'

No work from me! I who had kept all the accounts of the firm for a fortnight and entered all their letters in the peon's book, I to be told that to my face, when I felt certain that I had done quite as much as, if not more than, Mr. Pigeon had ever done in a month! An *éclaircissement* with Kinoo Báboo was now unavoidable. I taxed him with unfairness in not having reported to Mr. Pigeon all the assistance I had given him. He laughed outright. The sums I had worked out were all worked wrong, he said. The peon's book was ordinarily kept by a *sircár* on Rs. 8, who made the entries better than I had done.

The indignity was too great to be borne. It brought on fever, and I was laid up. I never returned to Messrs. Smasher, Mutton, and Co.'s office again.

CHAPTER II. FIRST EXPERIENCES IN THE TREASURY
Behold me six months after seated behind the counter of the Government Treasury, this time no longer an apprentice, but hedged with all the dignity that appertains to a paid servant of the Government.

What a grand sight for a young inexperienced man of eighteen! Rupees scattered on all sides in delicious confusion! Bright, *juloosee* rupees, quite new from the Mint! Small rupees—halves and quarters—equally bright and in heaps, in quantities which my inexperienced arithmetic had never before summed up. Gold—brilliant gold coins—with the quaint device of the lion walking majestically beneath the luxuriant date-tree—not in handsful, but in bagsful and in chestsful, which the mind could not have conjured up even in dreams;—there they were all before me scattered in every direction! I wonder who suggested the device on the gold-mohur. The date is an Indian tree, the lion an animal of Africa. Of course one can conceive of an African lion being left in a cage on Indian soil beneath the shade of a date-tree; but how could a lion at large be there, unless he had broken loose from the Barrackpore Park or some big ex-king's menagerie? I think the device should have shown a royal tiger under the tree, instead of a lion. To this the critic may object that the lion represents England's motto, which the tiger would not. True; but the correct conclusion from the premises is that the lion's proper place is on an English coin. On an Indian coin the tiger is more appropriate: and altogether, it is better that England should bear on her escutcheon two royal animals in place of one, being mistress both of the east and west. But lion or tiger it was the bright gold that arrested my attention, and I was in rapture for days.

And then the sound—'*chinck, chinck, chinck!*' Talk of the music of the spheres! What is it—what can it be—compared to the music of gold-mohurs and rupees? What soft variety too there was in the sound, gold giving out the most melodious '*chinck*' imaginable; silver, one just a shade harsher, but still so pleasing; while even bright copper rang out a tune that was not unpleasant! '*Chinck*! *chinck*! *chinck*!' on all sides. How the sound rung in my ears even in my sleep. For days, weeks, and months it haunted me as a pleasing fancy— a ravishing dream; till by every-day repetition it lost its charm, ceased to please, and ultimately became absolutely annoying. Thus even the sweets of life deaden the sense of pleasure by repetition!

There were other things also for a novice to note with wonder. The number of men coming in and going out; their faces, nationality, and the errands on which they came: these comprised a study in themselves. There stands the Jew—always and everywhere the most noted of men—with a large bundle of bank-notes (I am speaking of days past when there were no Government currency notes, but only notes of the Bank of Bengal in circulation) under his arm. What has brought him here? He has bought some chests of opium, and wants to send them off to China at once, and has come to pay down the price. There is the salt merchant scantily clad, redolent of mustard-oil, *chundan*, and putrid *áttur*, with his agent perspiring at every pore and tottering under the weight of a large bag full of rupees, waiting to have a pass for his salt.[3] The respectable English merchant is there, with his *sircár* by his side, to pay for salt or opium, or to invest in the five-per-cent loan which is about to be closed. The up-country *koteewál*, his mouth stuffed with *páwn* and spices, has come for money due on London bills. The sleek, oily Báboo has stepped in for the interest of his Government Promissory Notes. The peon of some great Civilian, with all the insolence which his master's position permits him to arrogate, is clamouring for the *tullub* of his master, which he insists on being first paid. Lieut. Sabertash, of H.M.'s 290th, wants the money due on a bill from Khámpteepore, and is about to create a disturbance on the plea of precedence.

The lieutenant in his red coat is a striking sight. He has lost his temper, and has not yet found his money. Why should he not be paid first? He is an officer of the British Army; do the *shroffs* and *keránis* know what that means? Not paid yet? He runs up to the Burrá Sáheb and lodges a complaint. The Burrá Sáheb is an old officer of much experience, and does not see what there is to complain of. The lieutenant must await his turn; 'first come first served' is the principle of the office, and cannot be departed from.

'What! not in favour of an officer of the British Army?'

'No!'

This is intolerable. Lieut. Sabertash comes down the staircase as fast as he went up. He is choking with rage, and must give vent to it. Ah! the unfortunate sepoy on duty! He has not got the bayonet fixed on his musket, in strict accordance to military rules. The lieutenant calls for the Subadár in command at once. This is his own independent element; no Burrá Sáheb can interfere with him here.

'Place the sentinel under arrest, and send him to the fort,' is the sharp order given; and the man is placed under arrest at once, and despatched to Fort William.

Simultaneously, the Burrá Sáheb writes to the Commanding Officer, to complain of the lieutenant's interference, and explains that in such a crowded place as the Government Treasury the bayonet cannot be kept fixed on the musket without causing accidents to the crowd. The sepoy is released forthwith; our deponent knoweth not whether the lieutenant got a reprimand for his interference. From the Treasury he drove off with a smiling face, like a victorious soldier from the field of battle.

CHAPTER III. HOW I GOT INTO FAVOUR

The alphabet of a cash office is easily learnt. 'Passes,' 'advices,' '*challáns*,' '*dákhillás*,' 'bank post-bills,' 'cheques,' 'interest drafts,' 'balance per contra;' all the mystery and enigma involved in those words were learnt by me in one week. The Burrá Sáheb was a good man, overflowing with the milk of human kindness, and was pleased to think kindly of me. A sort of indirect opposition to my appointment he had urged on account of my youth; but this gave way on his being told that I had a *moonsiff's* diploma in my pocket. The law lost a clever judge! But did not the Treasury gain a most clever cashier?

As I got initiated into the mysteries of my work, I felt that the poetry of the cash office, which had charmed me on entering it, was dying out. The music of bright rupees, and even of bright gold-mohurs, had long ceased to please, and the counting of bank-notes was a bother; but I was fast getting into favour, and that kept me in spirits.

Let me see; I believe it was in the time of the Áfghán War[4] that we were sending up lots of money North-west. We had placed a large sum on board a steamer, but the Captain had left without signing the usual receipt. The money had been in my charge, and the Burrá Sáheb had given orders to place it on board, and so I demanded a receipt from him. He smiled. Why was the receipt necessary? Was it not sufficient that he had given the order? Would any one hold *me* responsible if anything went wrong with the money? But I was firm.

'A receipt was the usual acquittance for money paid; and there was no reason why this particular case should be otherwise dealt with. Life and death were in the hands of God. What if the Burrá Sáheb died suddenly, and the Captain of the steamer bolted with the money? Possibly I would not be held responsible; but still I would have nothing to show that I had allowed the money to pass out under regular orders.'

I was afraid of my obstinacy, but the Burrá Sáheb took it in good part.

'If I don't give you a receipt,' said he, 'will you be dreaming all night that the Captain had bolted and the Burrá Sáheb was dead?'

'Possibly I might. I would certainly feel somewhat uneasy that everything had not been done in regular form, as usual.'

A formal receipt and discharge was thereupon given with a smile, and I rose vastly in the Burrá Sáheb's estimation.

Another cashier, an old man, was a bungler. It is necessary to explain to the uninitiated that all complete bundles of notes contain fifty pieces each. Of course all bundles in the hands of a cashier would not be complete, the surplusage of each description forming small bundles of from two to forty-nine notes. Well, on taking over the balance of the day one evening, the Burrá Sáheb came to a bundle containing forty-nine notes of 1000 Rs. each. The number was correct, and accorded with the figures on the balance sheet before him. But, just as the bundle was about to be dropped into the iron chest, old Goberdhone put in that that was a 'missing' bundle.

'What bundle?'

'Missing bundle, sir!'

The Burrá Sáheb counted the notes over again; once, twice, three times. The number invariably was forty-nine. He went carefully over the balance sheet; there was no mistake there even of a single pie. What then did the words 'missing bundle' mean?

'You say this is a missing bundle; what is missing? Is the balance not correct? Has any note been lost?'

'Oh no, sir! that is a missing bundle only.'

The patience of Job would have given way. I was at once sent for.

'What does this man mean by saying that this bundle is a missing bundle?'

I asked him to explain to me in *lingua franca* what he meant, and could hardly resist bursting out in laughter when he had told me.

'Well, what does the missing bundle mean?'

'Simply this, sir: it is a "miscellaneous" bundle, that is, formed of the accumulation of different dates.'

'Only that? then don't you allow this man to come up to me with the balance of the day again. Always bring it up yourself.'

Old Goberdhone was savage with me; but how was I to blame?

CHAPTER IV. THE ACQUAINTANCES I MADE

The Government Treasury is like a public mart, where one comes in contact with all sorts of people in the ordinary course of business. One day there came a young English cadet, with the bloom of old England still on his cheeks—the handsomest specimen of the human race that I have ever seen. He at once became the observed of all observers; there was a crowd around him; every one was anxious to exchange words with him. I thought he would get annoyed, there were so many after him at once. But with the sweetest face in the world he had also the sweetest temper, and he laughed and chatted with everybody without betraying the least impatience. If all Englishmen had been as even-tempered as that boy, would not the race have been idolized by the Bengalis? That cadet certainly was idolized on that day.

Unfortunately men of a different stamp are more common in the world. A young Marine apprentice, attached to the Pilot Service, I think, came a few days after, and exhibited the reverse side of the national character with great force. He also had some money to receive like the cadet, but would not exchange a word with any one and was impatient of delay. He lost his temper in no time, if it can be said that he had any at all to lose. Taking up a paper-weight of shots he struck one of the assistant cashiers with it, because his work had not been sufficiently expedited. The nigger, also a young man, was quite equal to the occasion. He snatched the paper-weight from the apprentice's hand and returned the blow with somewhat greater smartness. An Englishman on being struck always returns to his senses. He is apt to consider every man his inferior who does not establish by the incontrovertible logic of force that he is his equal. The young man behaved very quietly afterwards, but he never spoke a word with any one.

After experience has brought before me many repetitions of the conduct of the Marine apprentice. Elderly men, men of business, pious Christians, or at least men so famed, have all passed in review, and betrayed the same hastiness of temper, the same precipitancy in committing an outrage, the same submissiveness when beaten back; but in an experience of more than thirty years I cannot say that I have come across half-a-dozen examples deserving to be remembered along with that of the young cadet. The cadet of that day will be a general-officer now, but, the English army is so sparsely distributed over Her Majesty's vast dominions, that I have not been able to trace out his name.

I will now refer to another gentleman whom I also recollect with kindly feelings. He was an Áfghán—some relative of Sháh Soojáh,[5] he said—whom the British Government had agreed to shelter. He seemed to be every inch a gentleman, treated all men with courtesy, evinced the greatest affability in his manners, and was only wanting in gratitude to the nation of whose pension he was the recipient, but for whom he had no good word to say. I wish somebody would offer a prize for an essay to explain how the English nation, who are thoroughly honest, and are always anxious to do good, come to be misunderstood and unappreciated. With some this is owing to the foible noticed in the Marine apprentice; but surely all Englishmen are not of the same stamp. Why are they all alike disliked, if not hated?

CHAPTER V. HINDUISM *VERSUS* CHRISTIANITY

I was very much surprised one day to meet with an orthodox up-country Hindu who said he was staying at Spence's.[6] He said that he did not know anybody in Calcutta, and not knowing where to find accommodation had proceeded to the hotel for apartments. He of course did not take his meals there. For that purpose he went over every day to Burrá Bazaár—to the shops.

This gave me quite a new idea of Hinduism. In my youth and ignorance I had mistaken the orthodox dolts of Calcutta as representing the entire class of orthodox Hindus. I now found for the first time that Bengal had gathered a great many prejudices which were not entertained by Hindus elsewhere. What harm could there be in living in the same house with Europeans if you did not eat with them? what harm in sitting on chairs and lying on beds they had used? Northern India allowed all this; Bengal did not. I have since found still greater divergences on divers other yet more important points. No up-country Hindu carries his dying father and mother to the river-side; to them no place is better to die in than home. No up-country Hindu throws away his *páwn*, or lays by his *chillum* if there be a Mohammedan in the same *ghárry* or boat with him. No up-country Hindu when thirsty will refuse a glass of water from a leathern *moosuk*. And yet they are just as good Hindus as, if not better Hindus than, their brothers of Bengal.

In discussions on these points, which relieved the monotony of official work, we had a very good champion of Hinduism in a *mohurer* named Gungájal Báboo, an old *Vysnub* of great sanctity, who imitating the eccentricities of Krishna, had taken a second wife in his old age. He of course poohpoohed the orthodoxy of up-country Hindus, but being a *Vysnub* he was obliged in theory to cry down the restrictions of caste; and yet on this very point of caste he was a great stickler. The phases of Hinduism are so multiform that it is extremely difficult to reconcile them one with another.

The amours of Krishna were of course a prolific source of banter, but I shall never forget the earnestness of the old man when he explained the tenets of his faith with an unruffled temper. 'Krishna was—what? the same as Christ,—an incarnation of the *love* of God. *God is love*: the whole life of Krishna explains this, for it explains love in all its phases; love of the child for its mother, and of the mother for her child; love between friends; love between lover and mistress; love of the worshipper for the object worshipped.

What besides this does the story of Krishna expound? There are indecent anecdotes mixed up with it: reject them as spurious; they are the conceptions of indecent minds, connected, where no real connection exists, with a tale of great purity. What is the history of Christ'—would the old man emphatically ask—'but a repetition of the story of Krishna in another, but not a better form?'

I did not concede all that the old man contended for, but I fully believed in the purity of his faith, and to this day believe that salvation is not for the Christian alone, but for all who believe as this man believed, and who are true to their belief. I have a high respect for Christianity; but I have met with few, very few Christians indeed, entitled to greater regard than this man. A very respected authority had once heard a certain Lord Bishop explaining to his congregation what sort of a place heaven was: 'You will meet there with bishops and archbishops, deacons and archdeacons,' &c. Well, I have no objection to all the Lord Bishops being found there; but I feel quite certain— as certain as a human being can be on such a subject—that old Gungájal will be found there too, and perchance occupying a higher position than many bishops and archbishops.

Chapter VI. Chotá Sáhebs

I have spoken of the Burrá Sáheb of the Treasury, but as yet the reader knows nothing about the Chotá Sáheb. During my incumbency of about eight years there were four Burrá Sáhebs, and five or six Chotá Sáhebs; but of course it is not necessary to describe them all. As a rule Chotá Sáhebs everywhere are short-tempered young men, knowing nothing, who expect the *ámláh* to do everything for them, and at the same time to show them the same deference and respect as, or a shade more than, what is conceded to the Burrá Sáheb. There is no man who exacts respect more punctiliously than he who doubts his right to it.

But our Chotá Sáheb was on the whole a good man,—vain, as young men will be, flippant also, but not mischievously inclined. A fraud had been practised on the Treasury, and a small sum taken out on an interest-draft which had been paid before. The order of second payment bore the Chotá Sáheb's signature. At first his only fear was as to the view the Government would take of the matter with respect to himself; and his only thought was how to gloss over his share of the blame, and who to sacrifice as his scape-goat. Somebody suggested that perhaps the Chotá Sáheb's signature on the document was not genuine. This was a wisp of straw to the drowning man. He clutched at it with intuitive eagerness. 'Of course it is not my signature! Does it look much like it? I will swear in any court of justice that it is not my signature!" And so the difficulty was tided over, and the loss paid up by the *ámláh*. The Chotá Sáheb, freed from blame, was not unwilling to pay. But the amount was very petty, and the *ámláh* did not trouble him.

It was matter more serious when the Chotá Sáheb began to sign all sorts of papers that were brought to him. Somebody had to pay a large sum of money (eighty thousand Rupees, I think) into the Treasury on account of somebody else. He submitted the usual *challán*, or tender of payment, to the Chotá Sáheb for signature, the *challán* being accompanied by a receipt which was to be signed after the money was actually paid in. The Chotá Sáheb signed both simultaneously. There was the acquittance signed and delivered without a single pice of the debt having been actually realized! It fell to my lot to explain to the Chotá Sáheb his mistake.

'Mistake! what mistake? If I was not to sign the paper, why was it brought to me?'

'It was brought to you only for an order on the *challán* to authorize the cashier to receive the money.'

'Well, have I not signed that?'

'Yes, you have. But you have signed the receipt also before receiving the money. You ought to have waited for the cashier's acknowledgment.'

'Who is the cashier then, and why did he not send in his acknowledgment?'

'Because he has not received the money yet.'

'But why has he not received the money yet? Why did he not receive it ten days ago?'

'The payment was not tendered till now.'

'Bless me if I understand all this! What has gone wrong?'

'This only, that if the man had chosen it he might have gone away with your receipt without paying a pice of the money due from him.'

'Then let him go. He is welcome to do so, I suppose.'

The case was hopeless. There was no help for it now but to speak to the Burrá Sáheb, who of course understood the whole thing in two seconds. He kept back the Chotá Sáheb's acquittance, and told me to report to him when the money was received. An order was simultaneously issued and necessary directions given to the *chaprássies* that no papers were to be taken to the Chotá Sáheb for signature except by an *ámláh* of the office. But the Chotá Sáheb never attempted to understand what all this pother was about.

Another Chotá Sáheb, equally clever, did not understand why a gold-mohur, if equal to a rupee in weight, was so much smaller in size, and why bank-notes of different values had borders of different patterns when the paper used was the same. The difference between a cheque accepted and one unaccepted was also a poser; and it was mentioned of one Chotá Sáheb whom

I did not know, that he used to sign papers without looking at them, and every evening several blank papers and blotting sheets were to be found on his table signed in the usual way along with other papers. It must not be forgotten however, that these Chotá Sáhebs were generally very young men, paid to learn their work, and not expected to perform it efficiently.

CHAPTER VII. TROUBLES OF OFFICIAL LIFE—THE SINK-HOLES OF CALCUTTA

I have not yet alluded to the inconveniences of office-life, but the reader must not conclude that there are none. The inconveniences are many and of diverse kinds. I have referred to a fraud practised on the Treasury. The attempts made to discover the culprit gave me a lot of trouble. The man who had presented the duplicate order for payment was seen by me and by some three or four other assistants. The police, with their usual brag, said that they would trace him out without fail if he were in the land of the living, and the only little help they wanted was that of some sensible person to identify him. Of those that volunteered I was selected, and dreadful was the bother I had about it. I had to accompany the police through many of the dirtiest byeways of this dirty city, to nooks and corners where no decent person desires to be seen.

I was first taken to the house of a seal-engraver. In a hut was a squalid woman, with a thin squalid child on her lap. A policeman in plain clothes accompanied me, and asked the woman to fetch her husband.

'He is not at home.'

'Oh yes, he is; he told me to come for him. Tell him the Thákoorjee has brought some *maháprasád* for him.'

I did not understand what this meant; but the word *maháprasád* was evidently the 'open sesame' for admittance. The message was taken in; the man came out, more miserable looking, if possible, than his miserable wife and child. He was not the man we were looking out for. The policeman and he seemed to be old acquaintances, and they had a long talk of which I did not understand a word.

Next I was taken to the ground-floor of an old two-storied house, which was in a crumbling condition. There was a drinking party within, and they refused us admittance. The policeman in plain clothes did not come up to the house, but kept at a distance, another man being sent with me, who, I understood, was the friend or companion of the party to be identified. It would seem, therefore, that there can be no sort of real confidence between knaves. As admission into the apartments was refused, my companion began to bawl out for his friend by his nickname 'Kallo Ghose.' We were kept waiting for a long time, and curious eyes were peering out every now and then from a small aperture which represented a window, to see who we were and what we wanted. At last, after about a full quarter of an hour, Kallo Ghose came out. No: he did not come out exactly; he just opened the door partially and showed as his face. It was enough: he was not my man; but there was no doubt of it that he was a villain of the worst stamp. He asked my companion why he had brought another man, a stranger, with him. The reply was communicated to him by signs which I did not understand. The friends it seemed to me continued to be good friends still, but Kallo Ghose launched out any but kindly glances after me. If the mysteries of Calcutta[7] were written by a clever hand, we would know of many things which we do not dream of.

I was next carried to a flash-house kept by some unfortunate women, being accompanied by one who was a frequenter of it, while the police waited at the nearest corner. The time was immediately after nightfall; the abominations I had to witness were awful. Admittance was given without much demur. The party assembled were three men and two women; a third woman was lying on the floor dead drunk. There were two bottles of brandy or rum before the party, with several glasses; and they had one dish of *chabánás* also, with plenty of chillies. Of the three men one was a big quarrelsome fellow, with a red face; another, a very thin black man whom I was expected to identify; the third was a decent-looking fellow, whom I had seen before, but whom I did not know. The bully asked our business. My companion introduced me as a novice in the school of love.

'Does he drink?'

'No; but I shall drink for both.'

'That won't suit us; he must drink for himself;' and a glass of brandy was handed to me.

I refused it with thanks.

'Gulp it down,' said the bully, 'or I will force it down your throat. What business have you here if you won't drink? We transact no business with dry lips.'

I said that I had come there with my friend to see, but not to drink.

'To see what beasts we make of ourselves?'

My companion hastened to explain that I had only come to see the beauties of the house.

'That excuse won't pass with me,' said the bully. 'Whoever comes where I am, must do as I do. Now, sir, will you drink or not?'

'I won't.'

The bully began to gesticulate; but I knew I had only to bawl out for the police in case of need. This, however, was found unnecessary. The decent-looking person I have referred to asked me if I knew him. I answered in the negative.

'I have seen you before,' I said; 'but I cannot remember where or under what circumstances.'

'Do you know any of our party? Honour bright!'

'Honour bright! I don't know any one of you except him who has come with me.'

'Well, I know you, and the family you belong to. Give me your word that you will not mention our names, or in any way describe us to your friends, or mention in what plight you have seen us, when you go out.'

'This I can safely promise, because I do not know your names, and because my friends could not recognise you from any description I could give of you.'

'A direct promise, please; otherwise I won't interfere.'

I gave the direct promise required. He took the bully aside; I do not know what talismanic words he said, but the bully was at my feet in a moment, asking me to forgive his rudeness. Of course I forgave him. He insisted on shaking hands with me, and I was then allowed to depart; not without a pressing invitation from the ladies to come and see them another day.

In this manner I was carried hither and thither for some days, till the police admitted their inability to trace the delinquent.

CHAPTER VIII. THE BURRÁ HUZOOR—NATIVE SERVILITY

The rolling-stone gathers no moss. Be it so; but is the reverse always true? Here was I a stationary stone for years in the Treasury that had gathered no moss to speak of. We had better roll now, thought I; but in what direction?

The office of deputy-magistrate was being newly created. The first few appointments had been reserved for members of the highest native families in Calcutta, and for well-connected European candidates. But there were many others to give away. Unfortunately, I had no friends to back me; and those who I had expected would help me, did not. Young men, however, are not easily disheartened. The appointments were in the gift of a Secretary to the Government known far and wide as the Burrá Huzoor, and I waited on him to urge my claims. On the first occasion I was received and put off; on two subsequent occasions that I called I received the stereotyped answer— 'Phoorsut nehi háye.' There was the great man on whom all eyes were turned, the dispenser of bounties and coveted honours, accessible only to people with long names, and to such others as made 'koorneeshes' and 'salaáms' with both hands; but not to me and the like of me. I accepted my disappointment with impatience indeed, but still with as much pride as I could call up. Years after I had the satisfaction of receiving from the same man a message that he would be glad to cultivate my acquaintance, and, subsequently to that again, an offer of a deputy-magistrateship, which I refused. I can well conceive what Dr. Johnson's feelings were when he wrote that celebrated letter to Lord Chesterfield,[8] than which a better return below was never given.

In the height of his greatness the Secretary to the Government would not see me. I was delighted to learn some time after that a native gentleman whom he had asked to come to him had refused to do so. This was a gentleman of independent means and station in society, who cared neither for the favours nor the frowns of the great man. He had never waited on him, though all the other big guns of Calcutta had done so, and this was a sore point with the Huzoor, who liked to see rich natives about him. He took the initiative at last, and asked to see the Báboo on the pretext of consulting him on certain points connected with native female education. The reply was that on account of domestic bereavements the Báboo never went visiting. Oh! how the Huzoor must have felt the slight.

But against one instance of this sort how many there are of a contrary kind. The great ruling passion of the native mind is servility to those in power. All our Rájáhs and Báhádoors, with their *ássás* and *sontás*, are constantly running hither and thither 'to pay their respects' to this and that man—to every *topiwálláh* in office in fact, quite irrespective of his claims to such attentions. I can well understand when all this bowing and cringing originate with a purpose. Then the meanness has an excuse, possibly a knavish one, but still an excuse for the despicable position assumed. But I have never been able to understand why most of our purse-proud ignoramuses, who can have no ends to compass, go on demeaning themselves *ad nauseam*, crying, '*Jo Hookum*' to every puppy that writes C.S. after his name, merely as it would seem for that meanness' sake. When Báboo Hobo Gul Ghose goes visiting great folks in all directions we excuse him, because we know that the man is living on his wit's end. An up-country millionaire, with little or no brains, runs down to Calcutta with a long train of fancied grievances requiring the immediate attention of the Government; Báboo Hobo Gul is at once at his elbow, and offers to see him through the affair— for a consideration. The bargain is concluded without demur. Báboo Hobo Gul drives down to Government House; has an interview with the Private Secretary; even introduces his friend the millionaire to the Governor-General's right hand, without speaking of his grievances, as a matter of course. The millionaire does not understand a word of English, and it costs nothing to Hobo Gul to convince him that his suit has sped well, and that it is now only a question of money. The matter will be awfully expensive; there are so many big stomachs to fill. Of course the millionaire does not mind that, and a long fable ends with the demand of a large sum of money. But

Jumná Dáss Hurry Bhujun Dáss, though ignorant, is shrewd, and won't pay the whole sum at once. Half or one-fourth is after much haggling forked out at last; and Hobo Gul never appears before the millionaire again!

And yet these are the people to whom the doors of the great are always open; and the rich nincompoops who go there willingly bring themselves down to the same level with them. It is very seldom that an Englishman returns the visit of a native gentleman; yet my countrymen are too mean-spirited to resent this.

CHAPTER IX. TEMPEST IN A TEA-POT—THE ENGLISH OFFICE OF THE TREASURY

We were all very nearly losing our appointments one day, and that when we had not the remotest idea of such a thing happening to us. The Head Cashier had suggested some alterations in the general procedure of the office, with a view to provide greater security against frauds; but the Burrá Sáheb, a new man, had vetoed this, rejecting all the expostulations of the man who was primarily responsible for the proper working of the department. Our chief upon that submitted his resignation, which was at once accepted; and with him we all would have had to go out, as is usual on such occasions. But, simultaneously with his resignation, the Head Cashier had sent up a memorandum of his case to the Chief Secretary to the Government; and the Burrá Sáheb, just when he was about to fill up the vacancy, received the peremptory orders of the Government to leave matters undisturbed till a searching inquiry into the working of the office was made. For this inquiry a distinguished financier was selected, and it resulted in his unqualified approval of all the measures which the Head Cashier had suggested, and the removal of the Burrá Sáheb to a less onerous post. As the peons and duftries noted epigramatically on the matter: '*Burrá Sáheb bodlee hogyá; Báboo ká oopur Lárd Sáheb burrá khosee hooáh.*' The Burrá Sáheb's nominee who was to have filled up the vacant post of course flitted as fast as he had come; and the tempest in a tea-pot being over we breathed freely again, and continued working as before.

The new Burrá Sáheb was a thorough man of business, besides being a very pious Christian. He looked into every man's work with his own eyes, without neglecting his own. A great many checks and counter-checks were abolished by him, while he introduced various new ones in their place which were admitted on all hands to be exceedingly sensible and necessary. What did not give equal satisfaction was the selection he made in filling up vacancies. Even the best of men in some way or other manages to contract prejudices to which he steadfastly adheres. The firm conviction of this Burrá

Sáheb was that Europeans always made the best office assistants, after them East-Indians, and the natives last. This is even now the opinion of many very good men, and taken in the abstract the premises may not be unsound. But unfortunately no good Europeans are to be got for the salaries given in public offices; and if you stick to your hobby, the only result is that you cram your office with the refuse of Europe. As for the East-Indians, as a rule they are men of no education, and are therefore fit only for mechanical duties, and nothing more. The Registrar of the Government Treasury was an East-Indian, a very good man, and with the best education of the East-Indian standard. He had been many years in the office, and moved quietly in the groove to which he was accustomed. But he was entirely upset by the changes which the new Burrá Sáheb had introduced, and it was no secret that, in accommodating himself to them, he was wholly guided by the advice and direction of his native assistants. Like natives also (and after all what is an East-Indian but a native?) East-Indian assistants, when in power, bring around them all their brothers and brothers-in-law to partake of the loaves and fishes on the spread board. The English office of the Government Treasury had in this way become quite converted into a snug family conclave, consisting of three brothers, two brothers-in-law, one step-son, and half a dozen cousins of the first, second, and third degree. The Burrá Sáheb wanted to infuse into this *coterie* a little new blood. A good appointment was vacant, for which several excellent native candidates were applicants. But the Burrá Sáheb would fain have a European. At last a ship-captain recommended a nephew of his, a very young man, for the post. Of course he was totally unfit for it. But then he was a European, and—would learn. The lad had sense, but no education, and after a long schooling was barely able to get through his work as a matter of routine. He fell subsequently into bad company, took to the bottle, and got drowned. This of course the Burrá Sáheb could not have prevented: but he might have given the office a better man than the hobnail he put in. They say that the ship-captain was the Burrá Sáheb's friend, and had shown him and his family great attention on board when they came out. Was that a sufficient justification for the choice that was made? And yet there is no doubt that the Burrá Sáheb was a very good man and a pious Christian, as I have said at the outset. But prejudices, for or against, make the best men unjust at times, and the evil is that they don't see it.

Another selection made by the Burrá Sáheb at about the same time turned out much better. This was for filling up a comparatively unimportant post, carrying with it a much smaller salary. In this case also an English lad was selected; but he answered much better than the other man, being less bumptious and more willing to learn. For other very petty posts the Burrá

Sáheb brought in some natives who had served under him elsewhere, and all these turned out to be efficient assistants. But the appointment of so many outsiders caused great heart-burning in the office at the time, and made the Burrá Sáheb greatly unpopular, till his sterling good qualities developed themselves in due course.

Chapter X. The Supreme Court

The Jury nuisance is well known. I received one day a summons to dance attendance at the Supreme Court as a juror. Many cases where [sic] gone through. One was that of an indigo-planter charged with acts of cruelty and oppression against certain ryots. In the local court he had pleaded that he was a European by birth, and therefore not subject to trial by that court. His plea in the Supreme Court was that he was not a European and therefore did not come within the court's jurisdiction. The case was gone through, and all the acts charged against him were proved; but the court having left the question of jurisdiction to be settled by the jury from the evidence, the majority contended that the court's jurisdiction was not proved. To this the minority did not at first agree, but they afterwards gave in; and thus, curiously enough, the indigo-planter got off.

What struck me particularly in the court was that, though the show was a good one, the ends of justice did not seem to be fully attained. The interpretation was execrable. What the witness said was very seldom correctly rendered, and many things were put into his mouth which he did not say. The cross-examination of counsel seemed also often to be very irrelevant: but the counsel had certain privileges which they fully asserted and would not allow to be interfered with. There was a passage of arms between the judge and the counsel on this very point.

'You have been over and over repeating that question, Mr. Twigg. I don't see what you want to elicit. It seems to me that you are taking up the time of the court quite unnecessarily.'

'I beg pardon, my lord. But the question has been repeated so often most advisedly.'

'You may think so; I don't: and I really cannot allow this to go on.'

'Your lordship must excuse me. We have our respective duties in this court to discharge. Mine is to defend my client, and if by repeating any particular question I can throw one spark of light to clear him of the imputations made against him, I am bound to do so. And I hardly need remind your lordship that it is your lordship's duty and that of the jury patiently to receive the evidence as it crops up.'

'Very good, Mr. Twigg; you may go on.'

So the counsel had the best of it, and the judge was obliged to cave in.

As a rule the jurymen also were ill-chosen. Often, very often, native jurymen betrayed strong prejudice in favour of native offenders when belonging to the higher or middling classes; much oftener still, Christian jurymen openly exhibited their strong bias in favour of Christian culprits; and the right he had of challenging jurymen rendered it almost impossible for the court to convict an offender who was ably defended, as practically the choice of his judges was left with him.

In other respects, however, the court exercised a very salutary influence, especially in checking the irregularities of the police; and some judges took a delight in taking the officers of the police to task for any cause or no cause at all, of which the following is a veritable instance. The names of the jurymen having been called, the judge observed that the number of absentees was very great, and he fined the absent jurymen Rs. 20 each.

'My lord, I am present in court,' bawled out one juryman. 'My name was not correctly called out by the Clerk of the Crown, and I therefore did not answer, thinking that perhaps some other person was meant. If I (giving his name) was intended, I trust your lordship will, under this explanation, remit the fine.'

Mr. MacTurk, the Deputy-Superintendent of the Police, here nudged the juryman and told him in whispers that he must move through counsel.

'My lord, Mr. MacTurk, the Deputy-Superintendent of the Police, tells me that I must move through counsel; but as I am attending the court as a juryman, your lordship will perhaps kindly hold that to be unnecessary.'

Now, the judge, an irate man, was looking round like a mad bull, uncertain whom to gore. Was he to toss up the Clerk of the Crown, or the juror? Neither; the juror had found out the scarlet man for him.

'Mr. MacTurk, the Deputy Superintendent of the Police,' roared out the judge, 'had better mind his own business, which I have observed on divers occasions is very ill performed. He has nothing whatever to do with my court and my jurors, and I beg that he will interfere with neither.'

The silence in the court was profound; Mr. MacTurk was nowhere; all eyes were turned on him at once, but the ground had opened under him, and he had disappeared. Something the judge said to the Clerk of the Crown in an undertone which was not audible in court. The juror quietly elbowed up to the Clerk of the Crown, and asked him if his fine had been remitted.

'Yes, yes; you are very troublesome, B boo⁹. I shall take good care that you are not summoned again.'

And long did the juror bless his own temerity that had earned such coveted exemption.

CHAPTER XI. DRUNKARDS AND DRUNKENNESS

The vice of drunkenness has been making very considerable progress within the last five-and-twenty years. I do not mean to say that a quarter of a century before there were few drunkards. There were a good many even then; but there are a great many more now. Among my office-mates of those days, say out of one hundred men, I could count only about ten who drank at all, and of these two only were drunkards. A similar reckoning now would give fifty per cent. of drinkers, and at least eight or ten per cent. of drunkards.

I hate a drunkard. I hate even what cant calls moderate drinking. There is doubtless a great deal of truth in the saying that the good things of life are to be used, not abused. But I don't see that it can be made applicable to drink, not being able to understand that wine and spirits are 'good things' in the sense in which those expressions are generally understood, any more than ammonia, arsenic, and aconite. Very good medicines, but not very good 'things' any of them, I think. I don't want, however, to moralize. I want simply to describe the drunkards I have known.

The variety is very great; or rather the effect of wine and spirits is very different on different men. One will take his whole bottle of brandy, or one bottle and a half, (for these are the modern Bengali drunkard's usual doses,) very quietly, till he is fairly mastered, and finds his way to the gutters. Another will commence to become vehement before a quarter of a bottle has gone down, and wax more and more so as the doses increase, one whole bottle often failing to get the better of his fury. Of course both fellows are awfully disagreeable; but the latter much more so. The first only harms himself; the other, every one that comes within his reach. I cannot conceive of anything more villainous than for a man, knowing his foible, to go to the bottle again as before and then to abuse father, mother, wife, and children. Nor do they stop with abusing. Smash everything, whether it be a child's or a wife's head, a glass-case, empty bottles, or an earthen *handy*; smash everything and everybody that comes in the way. Behold the drunkard's jubilee!

Is Báboo Oghore Náth come to office to-day? Oh, yes; there he is: but he is high seas over yet, and will not be able to do any work. Has Rájendra Báboo come? No: he has been breaking all the furniture of his house last night; his wife has had a narrow escape; somebody else's bones were broken; his own hands and feet have been cut awfully, and he cannot come for some days. Now, should not some one have summary jurisdiction to prescribe a good dose of shoe-beating every time this occurs? A shoe-beating, mind, is the only treatment that effects a radical cure. There is no other remedy, and to my knowledge a good shoe-beating has never failed.

But how does the vice spread? It is so loathsome in its best phases, and the liquid fire is so hard to swallow, that one would think the infection would never catch. It does catch, though; and there are hoary villains who make it a trade to find recruits for the d—l's regiment. An old fellow of my acquaintance, and, sooth to say, a well-educated man, who once held a very respectable office under the Government, having drunk out all his substance and pawned his soul to the d—l, has to my knowledge been very assiduous in ruining others. Young men—younger, in fact, than his sons—were the victims chosen; the cloak assumed was friendship—great disinterested friendship—a real liking for the children—strong desire to do something for them in life—to introduce them into the highest circles, &c.; all springes to catch woodcocks,[10] and the woodcocks were caught. I don't know how the old scoundrel was benefited. He, of course, made himself a beast as often as he liked at the youngsters' expense; but that was all he gained. In the d—l's service men work very zealously on the smallest pittance; God's service requires more substantial bribes.

CHAPTER XII. OTHER BAD HABITS AND THEIR CURE

'Poor rule that won't work both ways,' as the boy said, when he threw back the rule at his master's head; and so the drunkard may say that all our philippics against drunkenness will tell just as well against other habits with which the bottle has no necessary connection. There certainly was one man among my office-mates who neglected his wife and children as much as, or more than, the drunkards I have named. He drew a decent pay, but not a pice of it went home. Friends told his wife to complain to the Burrá Sáheb, and she did so.

'Now, Jagganáth, what do you do with all your seventy rupees? Your wife writes to me that you don't pay her a pice, and she has to beg for her living and that of the children.'

'Oh no, sir; she has not to beg for it at all, sir. My brother supports her and the children.'

'But why should your brother have to support them when you are so well able to do it yourself?'

'I am not well able to do it, sir. My seventy rupees scarcely keep me afloat.'

'How is that? I thought seventy rupees to a man in your position was a good income. What does your brother earn?'

'Little enough, sir—'

'Don't try to blind me, now; let me know precisely what his pay is.'

'Sixty-five rupees, sir.'

'And what family has he got?'

'A wife and child.'

'Then his sixty-five rupees support six souls—himself, his wife and child, and your wife and two children; while your seventy rupees are scarcely able to meet your wants. How do you account for that?'

'Ah, sir! All men have not like wants—'

'Well, Jagganáth, you ought to be thoroughly ashamed of yourself; and now mind, if out of your seventy rupees you don't pay thirty rupees every month either to your wife or to your brother, for the support of your family, I shall strike out your name from the establishment list.'

'But, sir, I can't do it.'

'You can, sir, and you must. I shall make you do it.'

Now, what should be done to a man of this stamp, who, for the 'bought smile of a harlot,' sacrifices health, money, and domestic happiness, making life a burden to those whom he is bound by laws, both human and divine, to support and relieve? Here also a course of shoe-beating would be the best cure. Our forefathers understood this, and administered the medicine in sufficient doses to keep the family in order. But those patriarchal rules have now lost their force. Even fathers and guardians cannot now take the law into their own hands, and the consequence is unmitigated misery all round. There should be some one authorized to deal summarily with cases like these. The legal process of applying for maintenance and all that is too uncertain; and besides it does not cure the patient. I view both drinking and a bad life in the light of violent diseases which require violent treatment. My faith in the efficacy of the cure I have named is deep-rooted. The difficulty is in getting a doctor to administer it.

The word 'doctor' draws out a chain of new ideas on the subject. Do not several of our doctors (I mean our Bengali doctors) aid and abet the offenders—both by precept and example? I speak only of matters personally known to me. I felt sick myself and sent for a doctor—a countryman of mine. The complaint was a bad stomach, bad digestion, occasional pains.

'Oh,' says the doctor, 'no medicine is necessary. Take cocoa-nut milk—one entire cocoa-nut—after every meal, or take a bottle of beer.'

'But why beer, doctor, if cocoa-nut milk will do as well? The cocoa-nut will come cheaper and never make me tipsy.'

'What! are you afraid of getting tipsy, or have you really conscientious objections to the beer?'

'Very conscientious objections indeed, unless it be absolutely necessary.'

'Then the cocoa-nut will do just as well, perhaps better. But nine people out of ten would have preferred the beer.'

Doubtless they would, and therefore should the doctor be more wary in naming it. His is a high avocation, and he should not pander to the d—l if he can help it. If the beer be necessary, of course it is right that he should say so. But when such a harmless thing as the cocoa-nut will do as well, it ill becomes an educated man and a gentleman to suggest the use of that less harmless alternative which the giddy-pated are sure to prefer. We all have responsibilities in life. One unthinking word may light up a conflagration which all the waters of a whole river will not quench. I did not say all this to the doctor; but the thoughts occurred to me.

CHAPTER XIII. FORGERY TRIALS

A case of forgery has come up before the police magistrate, Mr. Bully, and my evidence is wanted. A Mr. Impudence has forged the signature of his brother, Mr. Stanley Impudence, the well-known aristocrat. I happen to know Mr. Stanley Impudence's signature, and am hauled up before the magistrate to say what I know.

'Your name is so and so? you are employed in the Government Treasury?'
'Yes.'
'Do you know the signature of Mr. Stanley Impudence?'
'Yes; pretty well.'
'"Pretty well" won't do. I must have clear and definite answers.'
'I know it very well then, your worship; exceedingly well.'
'How do you come to know it so well?'
'In the course of business.'
'Do for goodness' sake explain what you mean by such an indefinite expression as "the course of business," which may mean anything or nothing.'
'I have seen Mr. Stanley Impudence sign papers in my presence very often, and have observed the signature carefully.'
'Just look at the signature attached to this document. Do you recognise it as Mr. Stanley Impudence's signature?'
'No.'
'The name is correctly written?'
'Yes.'
'But it is not the signature you know?'
'No, it is not.'
'Is it like Mr. Stanley Impudence's signature?'
'No; there is an attempt at imitation, but not a successful one.'
'You would not pay money on that signature?'
'No, I would not.'
Here my evidence terminated. Similar evidence of others was taken, and then the case was sent up to the sessions. Mr. Bully was an excellent magistrate, but he liked to have scenes in his court: he was an old player who

had not given up his stage tricks on being promoted to the bench, and so he continued to act on to the end of his life. Our evidence in the case would not have been required, but that Mr. Stanley Impudence, who had refused to pay the forged cheque, did not appear to give his testimony about it, expecting, perhaps, that his brother might escape the clutches of the law if he kept back. My evidence and that of others who deposed to the same effect removed this hope, and Mr. Stanley Impudence, putting the best face on the matter, came forward at the sessions to deny his signature. Our testimony was therefore not taken at the sessions trial, but we had to attend all the same, lest friend Stanley should shy back.

Mr. Stanley Impudence and I were old acquaintances; but he cut me at the court, I suppose for the evidence I had given against his brother at the police. He stared me in the face; but I out-stared him. There was no chance of Mr. Stanley Impudence getting over me in that way. His brother was convicted and transported.

I saw another trial for forgery at the same sessions—the culprit in this case also being a European and of respectable connections. The Judge personally knew the prisoner and his friends in England; he said so in passing sentence on him. As there were no extenuating circumstances, he was obliged to pass the usual sentence of transportation, and the prisoner left the dock in hysterics. His friends afterwards succeeded in procuring a remission of a portion of the punishment, the local Government having the power to grant such remissions. Perhaps the young man deserved this kindness—perhaps he purchased it by his good behaviour. A similar recommendation in favour of a native offender—Sibkissen Banerjee—was not acceded to. I don't mean to say that Sibkissen deserved any show of kindness; but the recommendation on his behalf was based on equally good grounds, namely, age and good behaviour since transportation.

Chapter XIV. Assault and Battery

It is past 3 p.m.; some ten minutes after the time when the Treasury ceases to receive or pay money. An English woman (look at her bloated face and squalid dress; you cannot call her a *lady* even out of courtesy) runs in with a bill due at sight, and insists on its being paid. The *ámláh* are unable to comply, and she is referred to the Burrá Sáheb; but she has run out of breath, and is unable to go up. Go up she does at last; but the Burrá Sáheb is very sorry that he cannot help her.

'It is only ten minutes after three o'clock.'

'Yes, just ten minutes too late.'

'But surely you can pay me now quite as well as you could have done ten minutes earlier?'

'There must be *a time* to stop. If I pay you now, and another person comes five minutes after, how can I refuse him?'

'Mine is an exceptional case, Mr. —; I am a lady.'

'I am quite unable to accept the case as an exceptional one.'

'You are very unaccommodating. I expected greater civility from you.'

'Mrs. Horne, you are forgetting yourself.'

In great sulk the woman withdrew from the Burrá Sáheb's room. The cause of her importunity was soon made apparent. An old money-lender had lent her some money some months before. Neither money nor interest had yet been paid, and he had been put off for weeks and months. He then threatened to bring her up before the Court of Requests (now called Small Cause Court), and this she was anxious to prevent by paying down the interest at once. The bill had been shown to him, and he was willing to receive the interest in part payment without resort to law.

'Well, Mother Horne! have you got the money?'

'No, you stupid. These fellows here refuse to pay me to-day.'

'But I must have my money immediately. I have many dues of my own to pay.'

'Then go to h—ll and get the money. You don't get any from me.'

'I must get from you. You have put me off from day to day. You must pay the interest this evening, or I shall pass on to the Court of Requests.'

'I shall prevent you from doing that; I shall make you lame:' and no sooner said than done, she gave him a tremendous kick with one of her elephantine legs. The poor old man fell down much hurt. The bystanders took him up and helped him to the Burrá Sáheb's room, to lodge a complaint.

'What can I do for you, old man? I can't interfere in the matter. You should go to the police.'

'But, sir, she kicked me in your Treasury, and I complain to you. What else can I do? She is a lady.'

'I don't know what you can or cannot do. She is *not* a *lady*. If you had returned the kick, I would not have interfered. A woman that misbehaves in such a manner is not entitled to the privileges of her sex. But I cannot help you, old man. You must go to the police.' He did go there; but the police inflicted a nominal fine only.

There was another case of assault and battery within a short time after. A great Báboo—a millionaire—had come to the Treasury for interest due on his Government Promissory Notes. His carriage was standing at the door. An English gentleman comes soon after in his buggy, and tells the coachman to drive forward. This the pampered servant of a millionaire won't do. The

Englishman gives him a whipping. The Báboo's *durwáns* and *syces* surround him, and the Báboo himself runs out to the landing-place.

'You beat my coachman? Who you? Why you beat my coachman?' The gentleman tried in vain to explain to him that the coachman was to blame in not clearing out from the landing-place.

'I see you in the police. Why you beat my coachman? You know who I?'

'Don't make a scene here, Báboo. If you want to go to the police, I have no objection. But ask other gentlemen—ask the Báboos in the Treasury—everybody will tell you that the landing-place must be left clear for the last arrival.'

'But why you beat my coachman? tell me that;' and so it went on for some time, till cards were exchanged, and then counter actions were brought in the police. Of course, Lakhapati Báboo came off second-best.

Unfortunately these illiterate Báboos represent all native gentlemen in the estimation of Englishmen. They are insolent themselves, and teach their servants to be insolent. A part of the whipping that the coachman received might have been advantageously administered to the Báboo himself. The arrogance of Lakhapati Báboo sadly requires a cure. Education has done nothing for them; they have received no castigation at school; a little whipping now and then would be of inestimable service to themselves.

Chapter XV. Ugly Mistakes

I never received any reproof in the office but twice; once when I made a mistake myself, and the other time when I corrected one made by the Chotá Sáheb. It was on this last occasion that I learnt for the first time that men in authority make no mistakes. It was a glaring blunder that I pointed out. A debit entry had been made on the receipt side of the account sheet, and the totals of course did not square. All the items had been checked one by one, but as the amounts had agreed, the entry on the wrong side of the account had not been detected. More than an hour had been lost in this way by the *huzoor*, when, partly by guess and partly by intuition, I laid my finger at once on the item which required to be expunged from one side and taken over to the other. The Chotá Sáheb was furious. He first maintained that the entry was perfectly correct, and that my suggestion betrayed but little knowledge of accounts. I took the rebuke quietly, and by deducting the amount from one side of the account and adding it to the other showed that the totals came right.

'What then? That did not prove that a receipt was not a receipt?'

'No; but an examination of the voucher will show whether the amount was a receipt or a payment.'

'I did examine the voucher when I made the entry. Surely you don't mean that I make these entries at haphazard?'

'Of course, I don't mean that. What I mean is that, in the hurry of business, the entry that was intended for the payment register was made in the receipt register.'

'Absolutely impossible! I would consider myself unfit for any work if I made such a mistake.'

By this time other assistants had been going through the vouchers in the file, and, the one required having been found, it proved that my surmise was correct.

'I must have been very stupid at the time,' said the Chotá Sáheb, 'to have made the mistake. But how is it that you could not detect this sooner? You have been going over the account sheets with me for the last two hours. I, as having made the wrong entry, was not likely to discover the error; but you, as a looker-on, ought to have detected it at once.'

'It always takes some time to determine in what way a mistake of the sort would occur. It is difficult to detect such an error immediately.'

'Not difficult at all, I should say. If I were a looker-on, I could place my hand on it at once. I would do so by intuition. No great knowledge of accounts is necessary to detect a mistake of this kind. Your wits are not so sharp now as they used to be.'

It was useless contesting the point further with such a man. Instead of thanking me for finding out his error and relieving him of further trouble in the matter, he seemed to take a pleasure in blaming me for the delay in making the discovery, as if that exonerated him from the blame of having made the mistake. I therefore kept quiet, accepting the reproof as one of the many disagreeable but inevitable attendants of service. It is little evils of this nature that make service so unpleasant. They are not, it is true, of every-day occurrence, but they leave an impression on the mind long. A very great amount of forbearance and philosophy is necessary to override the petty evils of life.

I detected another more serious error of a different kind on another occasion; but this was an error committed by an office-mate, and the detection of it not only brought thanks but a handsome treat to the whole office. In paying a demand of Rs. 25,000, a brother-cashier, intending to pay it in five-hundred-rupee notes, had by mistake paid out 50 notes of Rs. 1000 each. The *mohurer* who assisted the cashier had also by mistake entered the notes as five-hundred-rupee pieces, but my eyes were caught by the borders of the notes (bank-notes of different values bore different border-marks), and I at once saw that something was going wrong; so I took the notes out of the *mohurer's* hands just as he was about to make them over to the payee, detected the error, kept back half the number, and had the necessary alterations made in the number book. The cashier was ignorant of all this at the time; the secret was kept between the *mohurer* and me, the surplus notes being retained in my possession. In the evening there was consternation and dismay, for notes to the value of Rs.25,000 were missing. The cashier was an elderly man, and I did not like to keep him long in suspense and misery, though I was advised by others to procrastinate. The notes were produced and placed in his hands. The old man was in ecstasies, and a treat to the whole office on Sunday following proved substantially the sincerity of his thanks. I allude to this matter only to juxtapose the conduct of the Chotá Sáheb with that of a despised nigger.

CHAPTER XVI. THE FREAKS OF FORTUNE

The wheel of fortune always goes round; but have we no hand in guiding it? Good fortune, I believe, is providential. We are often in luck's way, in spite of ourselves. But for bad fortune, who generally is more to blame than he who suffers from it? One old man took service in the Treasury on a salary of six rupees. Six rupees in those days was not quite so insignificant a sum as now, and yet it was small enough. Four rupees was peon's pay, and six rupees was barely above peon's grade; so that the man who did accept it, if of higher status, was undoubtedly of straitened means. This man that I was speaking of was of a good but poor family. In childhood a childless man of means adopted him, and dying left him, when he was about twenty years old, a small but decent fortune of a little above Rs.10,000. No sooner did the money come into his hands than he began to think how it could best be spent. The idea of keeping it and living on it never occurred to him. Advisers are never wanting when there is substance to swallow. Some suggested convivial parties, others Machooá Bazáar company, and interested parties gifts to Bráhmans and the like. But the young heir was an original genius, and had a hobby of his own to ride. He had seen tigers in menageries; he wanted to see how the lord of beasts stalked in his native woods at large. No sooner thought of than it was done. The idea was too bright and original to sleep upon. Boats were procured and manned with *páiks* and *shikáries,* and an excursion undertaken through the creeks of the Soonderbuns[11]. A large party had to be taken, because those creeks in past days were (and perhaps now are) infested by robbers, and the excursion was a somewhat prolonged one, as the feline monarch was not disposed to be very obtrusive. At last, after much bush-beating, a whelp somewhat larger than a pariah dog was seen—only for a moment, for he ran off to the higher jungles on becoming conscious of the proximity of man. The heir to another's fortune of Rs.10,000 was highly delighted; the one wish of his heart was now fully satisfied. His dream of dreams was realized; but the money had also slipped out, and he came back to the poverty in which he was born, and from which even Providence had tried in vain to rescue him. The subsequent history of his life is that of a constant struggle for the necessaries of existence, till in his old age he was obliged to enter the Treasury on the pittance I have mentioned, to discharge the duties of a subordinate *sircár,* scarcely distinguishable from those of a menial servant.

Another assistant of the Treasury whom I would here immortalize was a broken-down *poddár,* who in the heyday of his life had made a good deal of money by his profession, and more especially by the purchase of stolen goods. But what Satan helped him to, he also helped him through. The wealth thus acquired was spent in a manner equally, if not more, disreputable. He was a man of the old class, and not addicted to liquid fire; but he liked his *chillum* of *ganjá* and *churus,* and in his old age delighted to recount the number of frail women he had known. This garrulity was all the treasure left to him. He had not a pice in his pocket now; his clothes were tattered; he had no respectable relation who owned him; and, saddest of all, he had no wife or child to take care of him. He also had taken service in the Treasury on a pittance of six rupees a month; but his only regret now was that the females he had known—some of whom were still living—took no further notice of him.

A third acquaintance of the same class was a man of the weaver caste, who at one time had a good shop and flourishing business as cloth merchant in Natoon Bazáar. He was a very open-hearted fellow, and used to recount the stories of his own roguery with great glee. He had made some money in his day; but he led a cat-and-dog life at home, of which the presiding genius was a shrew. He could also never agree with his son, and between them all the money went out as fast as it had come, so that in his old age he was obliged to seek the sinecure's refuge in the Treasury on the same pittance as the others I have noticed.

CHAPTER XVII. A NEW BURRÁ SÁHEB

'Wherever you see a head, hit it,' was the advice of some son of the Emerald Isle to his English friend on introducing him to a regular Tipperary row. I have been trying to follow the advice to the best of my power, and have been hitting at every head right and left about me, without, however, doing aught in malice; and, till I am better advised, I intend to follow this course.

We had a good Burrá Sáheb heretofore in the Treasury, but Burrá Sáhebs are not fixtures, and the delineation of one does not necessarily describe all others. My old friend was a pious Christian, and a good man generally to serve under. His successor is a man of an altogether different stamp. But he is nevertheless a crack financier, and one thoroughly fit for the high post which he has been selected to occupy, except in one respect only, which I shall proceed to explain. In the round of pleasures that he has gone through, he has come in contact with all sorts of scamps—brothers and cousins of his fair acquaintances, pimps and go-betweens, broken-down hotel-keepers and keepers of empty-houses, and what not? All these people are of course beggars, loafers, or whatever else you may choose to call them. Their gay friend is now a great man at the Presidency, and he must provide for them all; and the old man is weak and silly enough to yield to their pressure. The former Burrá Sáheb had never perpetrated a jobbery in office, except in the one instance to which I have referred, when he appointed the son of a personal friend of his, a young and inexperienced fellow, to a post of great importance, in supersession of many experienced and deserving men. But the youngster in question was a respectable man, very respectably connected, and became in time a passable assistant. The new Burrá Sáheb filled up every vacancy as it occurred—not one or two, but a dozen—with men most disreputably connected, who never could make good assistants, but whose claims on him were such as he could not set aside. This caused great dissatisfaction in the office; but of course Burrá Sáhebs are not expected to care much for that. Is this an isolated picture of one high officer in one particular office only, or will the cap fit others? Keránidom would answer the question fully, if it could venture to speak out.

One of the assistants of the office had a small parcel containing books to send to England. It had been packed carefully in tin and covered over with wax cloth, when by accident it caught the Burrá Sáheb's eye.

'What business has that parcel in the Treasury?'

'None whatever,' replied the assistant referred to. 'It has only come with me.'

'What does it contain?'

'Books.'

'What books? I must open the parcel, since I find it in the Treasury.'

'I have no objection to your opening it, sir; only it will cost me a trifle to pack it up again, and I shall also lose the present mail steamer, as there would remain no time to repack it to-day.'

'I don't care; it must be opened;' and he took up the parcel, and carried it with him into his own room. Shortly after the owner of it was sent for.

'Now tell me truly what the parcel contains?'

'Books only, as I have said before.'

'What books?'
'I won't say that, because that is not my secret, but that of another person.'
'But when I open the parcel I shall know.'
'Open it then, and please yourself.'
'But is there anything within to please? Why don't you name the books?'
'I could not without the permission of a third party.'
'Am I right in thinking that you are packing off some indelicate books or pictures to England?'
'You are completely in the wrong, sir. Books of that description come out *from* England *to* this country, and don't go out from this country anywhere.'
'Is there anything within that would interest me in the slightest degree?'
'No.'
'Well then, you may take away your parcel; but, mind, never bring such things into the Treasury again.'

The man had, however, some good traits in his character. It is said he loved his wife to distraction, and went mad when she died. In a moment of temporary insanity he attempted suicide. His sirdar-bearer had suspected this, and stood concealed behind some almirahs, and when the master's hand was raised to blow out his brains, the servant rushed forward and laid hold of it. In the scramble the pistol went off, but hurt no one. The bearer secured a handsome pension for life. Very well, indeed, had he merited it! Call a nigger coward; it is the fashion to do so: but if this man was not brave (an unarmed man, attempting to disarm an armed madman), I do not know what bravery is.

CHAPTER XVIII. APPOINTMENT OF A NEW DUFTRY

A petty post in one of the departments of the Treasury had fallen vacant—viz. that of a *duftry* on five rupees. The candidates were many; a long line of Kháns and Meers stood ranged awaiting the arrival of the Burrá Sáheb, who wished to make the selection himself. During the incumbency of the former Burrá Sáheb there was a similar vacancy in the post of a *durwán,* with a similar parade of up-country athletæ. The selection in both cases was characteristic. The former Burrá Sáheb asked each man his name.

'Rámdeen Ojáh.'
'Ojáh won't do; I don't want a Bráhman.'
'Gugráj Doobay.'
'No Doobay for me: the same objection as to No. 1.'
'Mátádeen Tewáry.'
'I won't have a Tewáry any more than an Ojáh or a Doobay.'
'Luchmiput Chowbay.'
'The same objection as before. All Bráhmans are bad men, and I won't

have any.'

'But why do you consider them to be bad men?' asked the Chief Cashier.

'Oh, it is a lesson of large experience. I have seen that wherever a rogue is taken up, he is sure to produce his sacred thread; and I have seen also that the natives present invariably take his side, and try to get him off.'

'But that is only a rogue's trick. The rogue is not necessarily a Bráhman. He comes provided with a thread, simply that, if detected, he might be able to appeal to the religious prejudices of his countrymen, and thus secure a safe retreat.'

'Be it so. Then the man who has his thread by caste rights would have all the greater hold on the sympathy of his countrymen. I do not want such a man. You there, what is your name?'

'Lutchman Sing.'

'Ah! that will do very well. Sing means a "lion," I think. Well, I will have the lion. He is a good stalwart man, too. Let him be enrolled.'

The present Burrá Sáheb drives in in his buggy. All the Kháns and Meers make their humblest *salaám*. He does not even look at the men.

'Just read over their names.'

The names are read over. One, two, three, four; he shakes his head in disapproval. The name of the fifth is Shaik Baichoo.

'Stand forth, Baichoo! Have you worked anywhere before?'

'Yes, Huzoor; in the Busy Khána for two months.'

'Very good, that will do. Let him be appointed.'

Baichoo's maternal uncle is a 'Háfiz,' who made a pilgrimage to Mecca, and now keeps an empty-house in Chunam Gully.

The subject stinks; and the reader has had enough of it already. The Burrá Sáheb works very hard, and, taken all in all, is not a bad office-master. When he does take the side of a worthy man, he supports him thoroughly, and no amount of opposition from higher quarters ever made him forego the side he had taken. To the public he is more accommodating than his predecessor. There is no precise adherence to three o'clock with him, and ladies and Lieut. Sabertashes always get their work done with great expedition. At the same time, he does not allow the public to crow over his subordinates. Some irascible son of Neptune had threatened to kick a *poddár* if his cheque was not attended to at once. The *poddár* reported the matter to the Burrá Sáheb, who told him not to pay the money till after everybody else was paid. Neptune Junior remonstrated. 'I shall hand you up to the Government if you say another word,' was the reply.

CHAPTER XIX. SUNDRY MILLIONAIRES

If I have hurt any one in the short but brilliant chapters I have written, let him send me a new *pugree* or *chogá,* and I shall forget the past. Such, in the words of Joe Miller,[12] slightly altered, should be my answer to all Burrá Sáhebs and Chotá Sáhebs who may feel aggrieved at what I have written. The public at large I have generally treated respectfully, with occasional exceptions here and there. But there must be many more exceptions in the pages to follow.

I remember that I have already described one millionaire. I can recall to mind many others whom I have known. One was a fat fair man, about forty years old when I first saw him, who fed well and dressed well—both in the native fashion—and was the owner of some ten lakhs of rupees, the interest of which he would come to the Treasury to receive. He did not know how to read and write, and, instead of signing his name, was content to put down his x mark. Bless me! he did not know even how to speak. To every question he smirked in reply, and the *sircár* at his side was obliged to explain what he meant. The man seemed to be very good-natured though, and I dare say accepted the evils of life resignedly. Even ten lakhs of rupees, with stupidity like his, would perhaps be regarded as an unbearable evil by some, and, if allotted apart from the good nature given to him, would perhaps make many mad. But he took the infliction very quietly; ate, slept, and was merry in his own way, as an orthodox Hindu.

Millionaire No. 2 whom I remember was equally illiterate. He also did not know how to read and write, and did not sign his own name; but he was of the genus 'Young Bengal,' from the tassel of his cap to the tip of his boots, and always dined at Davy Wilson, the baker's.* The whole aim and end of existence to him were comprised in dressing smartly, dining at Wilson's, and driving out in the course to stare at ladies. Where he slept the d—l only knows. They say that Sibkissen Banerjee, the convict I have referred to in a previous chapter, once gave him a smart whipping, because he wanted to have the precedence of him somewhere. The place need not be named. Sibkissen was then in the height of his impudence, and the millionaire had the worst of it. He drank out his fortune, and left his widow a beggar.

Millionaire No. 3, when I knew him, was a young man—scarcely above twenty-five. He had been once at school, but, of course, had learnt nothing beyond being able to order hot tiffin from Wilson. The one sole object of his life was to have a new mistress every day, with wine and *tamáshá* in her company; and each new day was an exact repetition of the days past by, with such incidental variations as chance brought about. Over the wine-bottle he

* Now known as the 'Great Eastern Hotel.'

bet with a chum that his companion for the day was the prettiest woman in the town. His friend maintained that he knew another who was prettier. A wager was laid. The two scarlet ladies were brought together; their admirers retained their respective opinions; hard words were exchanged; the wine-bottle was triumphant; and the millionaire got well kicked. But he did not lose his friend for all that, the very slight disagreement between them, which only ended in kicking, being easily made up next morning. Are these overdrawn sketches? They are taken from the life, the name of the parties only being withheld.

Millionaire No. 4 was a Young Bengal in days past, but became an Old Hindu towards the termination of his career. He was a person of parts, and went through a splendid fortune, contracted debts, got cured of his follies, entered a profession, and amassed another fortune bigger than his old one. He all at once donned the appearance of respectability, made his *poojáhs* with great parade, and affected to be a representative man of the highest order. But he was old Satan himself under his clothes; kept a venerable pimp in his pay; cheated right and left, notwithstanding that he already possessed more money than he knew what to do with; and finally completed his misdeeds by leaving his son a beggar. He was the only rich man with a very cruel heart that I know of. Just before the Treasury a poor cooly with a heavy load on his head fell down before his carriage; the driver pulled up; the carriage stood still, but only for two minutes, to allow the cooly to get up. The great man within was in a terrible passion; he ordered the poor cooly to be well whipped; two or three cuts were given to him, when the bystanders—one or two European gentlemen from Spence's—interfered so vigorously that the coachman was obliged to desist.

Ah! my masters! This is a very bad world to live in, and a poor *keráni* sees very little to envy in those who are placed above him—especially among millionaires, who make so much fuss in the world. An acquaintance of mine, who had a name at school, and joined the mercantile line when I became a *keráni,* is now a beggar in the streets, simply from having kept company with millionaires, and contemned all humbler fry. I would rather be a dog and cry 'Bow wow' than go after a millionaire, that I may be taken for a great man too.

CHAPTER XX. SCRIBBLING VINDICATED

'Come, boys, let us leave off work and go to sawing wood,' as the blacksmith proposed to his apprentices, who were grumbling over the task he had assigned them; or, as the farmer said to his hired men, 'Let us play digging cellars by moonlight after the day's work is done.' This is very good advice to follow, particularly for young men, who, if they are lazily inclined, are sure to go to the bad. Excluding office hours, there is plenty of idle time hanging on most of us, and we must find occupation for them, or some other gentleman is sure to forestall us. Work! work! work! It is the condition of our existence, and we must abide by the condition manfully. Nothing is more painful or more tedious than to be idle, and nothing can be more dangerous.

To the above sage advice, which is not a very new one, I will add a sager maxim, which also has run many editions, that every man who minds his own business, without troubling himself about that of other men, can always create for himself plenty of work to keep him well employed. In this respect, an office-mate of mine set all of us a good example by selecting for himself the idle trade of a scribbler. Yes: the trade is called an idle one, and is so to this extent, that it brings no money to the till; but it never fails to find full employment for those who seek it; and it carries with it its own reward—as well as its own punishment also! And so the person I refer to found it; and so others will who follow the good example. He began by tagging verses, and spinning out long yarns in prose, on all and every subject, merely to kill time; and long columns of prose and verse began to appear regularly, week after week, in the Saturday-evening papers with his full name attached to them, he being then at that age when people fancy themselves to be unusually clever, and are particularly anxious to see their names in print. Of course his effusions were nothing to speak of; but he did not think so, and, besides keeping him well occupied, they did him the great service of introducing him to the public at large, which eventually was of much benefit to him. One or two very clever men, high in the public service, were pleased to see something in them, not exactly of merit, but of indications of future usefulness; and this encouraged the writer to go on, though young fellows like ourselves, who envied him vastly, lost no opportunity to disparage his efforts, irrespective of the private feeling which we felt was gnawing up our vitals. He was not, however, to be easily put out. His success increased with his years; and eventually the magazines and reviews were glad to accept his contributions.

This young fellow, like me, had no friends to push him on in life; but his scribbling did that for him which his so-called friends would not. The head man of an Account-office, who had noticed his writings on several occasions, was pleased to think that he would do particularly well as an assistant in his department, where there was plenty of letter-writing; and from the chrysalis state of a Treasury-clerk he was at once converted into a veritable *keráni*. Among the papers of recommendation produced by him was a letter addressed to 'Douglas Bennett, Esq.,' written by the editor of the best magazine of the day, advising the transmission of a cheque for a specified amount in payment of a particular contribution.

'Who is this Mr. Bennett?'

'I am Mr. Bennett, sir,' was the prompt reply.

Mæcenas smiled, and the appointment given to the young man on probation was at once made *puccá*. Oh! how I envied his good fortune! and did I not teaze all my friends that I was not equally lucky! For weeks and months I screeched about like a madman, disparaging the merits of the man who had succeeded, and cursing Mæcenas[13] who had failed to discover my superior worth. Such is friendship! Such is life! At last, as chance would have it, I too was successful, and, success curing envy, I bade adieu to the Treasury with hearty good-will, and joined my old office-mate in his new office, once more as a friend, under the respectable designation of an examiner, from which grade I was sometime after promoted to that of a drafting-clerk.

CHAPTER XXI. THE REGISTRAR

Now, then, for reminiscences of the Account Department, which I shall begin by introducing to the reader the Registrar of our new office, Mr. Milk-and-Water, a very quiet gentleman—exceedingly fussy, but absolutely harmless. He did not understand any work himself, nor did he pretend to do so. In the struggle he had for bread, he tried his hand at everything, from indigo-planting to the occupation of a broker; but he did not succeed in any. When put to his wits' end, he thought he would make the best of his stalwart person, and, with this view, entered the service of a gentleman high in the public service on a very small pay. Mrs. Percy soon took a liking for her husband's personal assistant, and when Mr. Percy died some years after, Milk-and-Water stepped into his shoes without any difficulty. A Civil Servant's widow always has many friends, and Mrs. Milk-and-Water had only to ask to get her new husband his present high post. Is not this a nice way of getting on in life? Only very few persons have the necessary qualifications.

I knew of another very similar case in which an East-Indian assistant on small pay got into the good graces of his master's wife, and associated with her after her husband's death. Here there was not the same success in life on the part of the lady's favourite, first, because the living together was a great scandal and drawback in itself, and, secondly, because the fellow had no ambition, being quite content to spend the lady's fortune (a very handsome one), which she, with a fatuity common under such circumstances, allowed him freely to squander. This man held a small post in a Government office. He died a sudden death, they say, in his sleep, while in the arms of the woman who loved him so dearly.

Well, Mr. Milk-and-Water's fitness for the post he held need not be further discussed. He did hold the post, and no man who had the good fortune to work with him ever complained of it. He knew his own shortcomings well, and never tried to lord his authority over those below. Of course he was fussy—very fussy, as I have stated. How can the head of an office, who does not understand his own work, preserve the respect of his subordinates without being fussy? 'Do this,' 'Do that,' 'Is the work done?' 'Quick, please'—to assistants; and to the Burrá Sáheb (Chief Accountant)—'Oh! I shall see this done, sir,' 'This will be attended to at once,' 'The other work you will get in no time,'—was all he had to practise every day. With most Burrá Sáhebs this was enough. So long as the work was done, they cared little who did it; and inefficiency at the top is, as a rule, seldom a defect to note upon. It is inefficiency at the bottom, or towards the bottom, that is always critically observed. Occasionally, however, Mr. Milk-and-Water caught it, and I was an accidental witness of this one occasion. The Burrá Sáheb had got very angry over something which old Milk-and-Water had not been able to explain. I do not know what the matter was. I had been simultaneously sent for about some other work, and only came in to hear the last part of the great man's rebuke.

'Mr. Milk-and-Water, I see you can't understand anything. You are absolutely fit for nothing, sir. Very well, you can go now.'

After this my work was disposed of, and, when I came out of the Burrá Sáheb's room, I saw Milk-and-Water waiting for me near my desk.

'This is an office of humiliation,' he said; 'see to what an office you have come with your eyes open. I dare say you were much better off where you were. But pray don't let this matter circulate like wild-fire in the office.'

'Certainly not; don't think me so indiscreet.'

CHAPTER XXII. THE SHOE QUESTION DISCUSSED—SOME OFFICE-MATES DESCRIBED

In the office to which I now belonged, the East-Indian element was very strong, much stronger than the native element, and the new appointments of myself and my friend were regarded by the former class as a poaching on their preserve. The fact is, the Burrá Sáheb who selected us had taken into his head the idea that the work of an Account-office could be done better by natives than by East-Indians, and we were especially selected to give his experiment a trial. The class of natives hitherto in the office belonged to the old school, though there were one or two among them worth more than they passed current for. Of the rest, one instance will suffice.

In going to the Burrá Sáheb, I of course always went with my shoes on. I was surprised one day to find another native assistant, of an equal status with myself, standing before the Huzoor with bare feet. When we both came out, he gave me a lecture on the disrespectfulness of my conduct in not taking off my shoes. I did not, however, see in what the disrespect consisted, and said that to my mind the disrespect was in going in with bare feet. This made him very angry, and he called together a committee of all the old native assistants of the office, who were unanimous in condemning me. I refused, however, to accept this decision.

'Has the Burrá Sáheb ever asked any of you to take off his shoes?'

'No; why should he? or how could he, when we never gave him the opportunity to do so?'

'Is there any order, written or verbal, requiring that shoes should be taken off?'

'None of recent date; but there was such an order in times past.'

'Which has now become obsolete?'

'Well, not exactly. People who want to show their respect for the Burrá Sáheb always observe it still.'

'It is just there that we differ, my friends. You observe the practice as a mark of respect. That doubtless was the view taken of the matter many years ago, when the order you refer to was passed; but it has long ceased to be so regarded by civilized men. At this day, they regard bare feet as a studied mark of disrespect, and it is for that reason only that we never pull off our shoes now.'

'But suppose the Burrá Sáheb were to take notice of your recusancy?'

'Of course if the Burrá Sáheb orders me to take off my shoes, I shall do so. But I don't expect such an order, any more than I expect an order to pull off my trousers; and, in the absence of peremptory orders, I consider it more respectful to keep on both trousers and shoes, and shall continue to do so.' They looked daggers at me, but I was not further molested.

The East-Indian assistants also were, for the most part, inimically disposed towards me; mainly because, as I have already stated, they thought that I had no business to be in that office at all; and, moreover, because I did not cave in to them as the other native assistants did. There were two exceptions among them, however, whom I cannot but remember with thankfulness. One was a literatus of some standing, who had made himself a name by his contributions to magazines and annuals. He welcomed me with open arms as a personal friend, though he had never known me before; helped me with his experience in the office, whenever I had occasion for such assistance; and proved himself every inch a gentleman, quite above every feeling of rivalry or class antipathy. The other was also an educated man, but not possessed of an equally good heart. He, indeed, sided with me, but only because I was the

Burrá Sáheb's nominee, and he thought that the best and safest course for him to follow was to pull with the current with a good grace.

It is scarcely necessary to notice any more of my office-mates at this moment. They will doubtless, many of them, turn up in the course of the narrative, and I promise to depict each faithfully as he comes forward. As the Irish magistrate mentioned from the bench, I shall always take care neither to be partial nor impartial in dealing with them. I can say of them generally, what Johnson said of the Scotch—I don't hate them, nor do I hate frogs, though at times I am obliged to regard them as very unnecessary evils.

CHAPTER XXIII. VISITORS AND OMEDWÁRS

It will be understood from the notice I have taken of the treatment Mr. Milk-and-Water received from the Huzoor that the latter was not a man of a very even temper. He was nevertheless not a bad man: far from it; taken all in all he was a very good man to work under, one who did his own work conscientiously, and always showed a liking for those of his subordinates who worked well. He took a particular fancy to me, gave me a room adjoining his own, and befriended me in divers ways on divers occasions. What he was most fond of was work, constant, unremitting work, without rest or respite; and what he did not tolerate was being interrupted in his work. One day a smart young man, neatly dressed in Young Bengal fashion, with a new shawl turban and new patent-leather boots, came to see him. The usual glazed card was sent in, and the visitor sent for.

'Take a seat. What do you want?'

'Come to pay my respects, sir.'

'Very good; but what else? Is there anything particular that you want to be done for you?'

'Yes, sir; give me an appointment, sir.'

'Why, Báboo, we are making no appointments now; there are no vacancies to give away just at present. But you can send in your application, stating your claims.'

'Yes, sir; but will you give me a good appointment in the Department; a fat, gazetted appointment, sir?'

'I really can't say anything at present. I shall submit your application, when I receive it, to the Governor-General for orders.'

'Very good, sir.'

'Good morning to you, Báboo.'

'Yes, sir.'

'You can go now; you see I am very busy.'

'Yes, sir,' again replied the Báboo, but without stirring from his seat.

'Do go, Báboo; will you?'

'Yes, sir,' and he rose from his seat, but stood fast behind the chair.

'Well, what more do you want?'

'Nothing, sir.'

'Then go, please.'

'Yes, sir.'

'My goodness! why don't you move?'

'Yes, sir.'

Short Temper could hold out no longer. 'Will you go or not?—*Qui hye, Báboo ko nekál dayo.*'

This, the reader will say, was an ignoramus, demeaning himself as ignoramuses will. Yes; just so; but unfortunately these ignoramuses are very plentiful in every grade of life, and bring a bad name on all natives generally. A Deputy Magistrate, while in a boasting mood, related to me how he had forced himself *nolens volens* on the notice of a Judge of the High Court. He came to our office very early one morning, when I and a few other assistants only had dropped in.

'Hollo! Deputy Sáheb, what brings you here so early? Has there been any difficulty in passing your salary, or any mistake discovered in your accounts?'

'Oh! neither; I have just dropped in on my way back from Garden Reach, where I went to see Mr.—, the High Court Judge, at his residence.'

'I suppose he receives visitors only in the morning?'

'Well, no; the fact is he receives no visitors at all. I called another day in the afternoon, and was refused. I asked his Jemádár when the Sáheb was comparatively idle, and learnt that he did nothing in the morning besides reading the newspapers, but that even then he did not receive visitors. I was determined, however, to see him, and went this morning. I sent in my card, and what does he do but write on it—"On what business?" I replied—"To pay my respects." The *chapprássie* brought back the usual reply —"*Phoorsut nehi háye.*" I did not know what to do. Shortly after I heard the Sáheb ordering his *ghárry*, and I waited for him at the landing-place. How was he to avoid me now? I stopped him just as he came down the staircase, and I kept him full one quarter of an hour standing there and talking to me. Nothing like perseverance, you know.'

'But had you anything particular to tell him? Did you know him before?'

'No, I did not know him before; nor had I anything particular to say. But I make it a point to call on all these great folks, and make friends. You don't know when they may be of service to you.'

Can a character more despicable than this be conceived? Mind, the man was a so-called educated man, and held an honourable post in an honourable branch of the public service.

The Huzoor of the Account Department never refused to see any one. He had only no leisure for idle talk. Sensible visitors took the hint he always gave them. One idler, after a short interview, was told by him that he was very busy.

'I can call another day when you are less so.'

'Oh, Báboo, I am always very busy.'

This was enough for the person I refer to; he never came again: but the hint does not operate on others in the same way. One brave Rájáh in particular vexed the Huzoor out of his life. Him he could not well turn out as he did all meaner fry, and the fellow took advantage of this and came to him very frequently—every time with a new favour to ask. He compromised me, too, with the Burrá Sáheb to some extent. Seeing that I sat by myself so near to the Huzoor, he took me for his special favourite, and thought I might be able to help him; so, after seeing the Huzoor, he made it a point to see me. While in my room, he would often become so uproarious in his mirth as completely to upset the Huzoor's equilibrium in the adjoining apartment, and the Huzoor thought me partly to blame for encouraging his visits; though I, of course, could not have kept him out, even if I had tried to do so.

CHAPTER XXIV. HUZOOR NO. 2 AND HIS FRIENDS

The Chief Accountant was a very good man; but Accountant No. 2 was the reverse. He hated natives, and was exceedingly foul-mouthed. I had nothing to do with him especially, the Burrá Huzoor having selected me as his personal scribe; and it was very fortunate that it was so, as I could not possibly have agreed with No. 2. He also had a favourite in the office, but that favourite was quite as afraid to approach him as anybody else; and even visitors were treated most rudely by him. My contiguity to the apartments occupied by the Huzoors enabled me to note all that passed in his room. During some vacation or other there was a rush of Mofussil officers 'come to pay their respects' to the Huzoors. They easily found admittance to the Burrá Sáheb for short interviews; but the case was very different with No. 2.

'Hámjántá háye. Sállá lok ká choote millá háye. Bullo Sállá lok ko, hámárá phoorsut nehi háye.'

Of course this was between the Sáheb and his peons. If he had dared to abuse the officers in their hearing, he would have surely caught it, as doubtless some one or other would have had the courage to hand him up to the Government, and abuse is the last thing that the Government will tolerate. If I remember aright, some Mofussil officer was for such offence degraded and warned.

The friends of our No. 2 were also apparently of the same feather. One of them, in coming up the staircase, was accosted by a clerk of the office by mistake as a brother-assistant, with the cordial 'Hollo! Robinson,' and a slap on the shoulder. The Sáheb was running up the staircase while the assistant was running downwards, and they found themselves looking at each other with very different feelings when one was at each extremity of the stairs. The assistant had already discovered his mistake, but was puzzled and did not know what to do. If he had only run up and apologized, there would have been an end of the matter. This he did not, and the irascible Sáheb, not receiving the apology he was expecting, ran downstairs, chased the assistant all over the first floor of the office, and gave him a tremendous caning. I don't blame the Sáheb much for this, for he was a young man then, and hot-blooded: but it ought to have occurred to him that the man who had slapped him on the shoulder as an office-mate could possibly have no object in doing so purposely, and must have done it by mistake. Fortunately for the Sáheb, the assistant he fought with was a short, puny fellow, who accepted the thrashing quietly. The result might have been different if he had had a hardier man to deal with, and therefore was the Sáheb's action exceedingly indiscreet.

CHAPTER XXV. SUCCESS IN OFFICE AND OUT OF IT

Shirk work is the great secret of an account office, as probably of all other offices also; and when the head man, like the Registrar I have described, does not understand his business, this is easily done. My cue from the commencement was to take up as much work as others chose to shirk, and I never had cause to regret this. Of course it was painful to be constantly grinding away, when others equally placed had plenty of leisure and holiday. But the day of reckoning came. The Burrá Sáheb saw what I did; the experiment he had taken in hand had fully succeeded; and I was rewarded to an extent for which there was no precedent. Then arose a cry of rage and disappointment from all sides, and this took the shape of a round-robin remonstrance addressed to the Huzoor by all my seniors, some nineteen in number, whom I had superseded. But they had mistaken their man altogether. The Burrá Sáheb sent for all the recusants, returned their remonstrance to them, and said that, if it was not forthwith withdrawn, he would be under the painful necessity of dismissing the whole of them at once. Of course all this tumult did not make me a favourite in the office; but my success, such as it was, quite reconciled me to the discomfort of my lot. This, however, was the only promotion I ever received for many years, and, though I was never actually superseded, I saw people on all sides of me afterwards getting on better in life, and never could understand how I came to be left in the lurch. One thing I never did—I never cringed to any man for a favour.

The experiences I had in this office are of a varied character. Those who got out of it, I found, generally fared well in life; but those who stuck to it stuck in the mire. One European assistant left the office and became a horse-dealer in Australia, made a fortune there, lost the whole of it again–the d–1 only knows how—came back to the office, left it again for Australia, where, when I last heard of him, he was said to be doing excellently well. Another European assistant was sent away for some fault, and became a tea-planter, and then an indigo-planter, and is now said to be worth some lakhs of rupees. A third assistant, an East-Indian, joined the Police Department, where he is doing exceedingly well. A fourth gave up his appointment to join his father's business of a hotel-keeper at a distant sanitarium, and is said to be worth plenty of money now. A good many others were pensioned off, of whom one has become a man of substance by private enterprise; another is doing still better by service under other masters, his perquisites being greater than his pay; and another is fighting with his wife, with whom he has all along been living a cat-and-dog life. Of the native assistants, one went out with a fat appointment to the Mofussil, where he has earned well-deserved honours; another was most fortunate in obtaining a fatter appointment in Calcutta, to which he is still attached; a third, who held a very petty post in the Account Department, went out on a fortune-hunting expedition on his own account, was taken in favour by some silly up-country Ránee whose faith in a Calcutta Báboo happened to be implicit, fleeced her and her minor children handsomely, and came down laden with booty, the envy of gaping thousands! A fourth and fifth have died, one in the prime of life, both exceedingly regretted by those who knew them.

CHAPTER XXVI. BÁBOO MÁDHUB DUTT

The office building was private property. It belonged to a millionaire, who used occasionally to call over personally to inspect it. I have immortalized a good many millionaires already in these pages, but this man was of so different a stamp that I am induced to foist him in also. We did not know each other personally before; but he came and introduced himself as well-acquainted with the seniors of my family. He was an old gentleman of very unostentatious manners; I may say, having about him almost the simplicity of a child. The race is dying out. We find very few men like him now. Of him an excellent characteristic story is told. He had a good *bazaár* which brought him a handsome income. Another rich Báboo set up a rival *bazaár* in the neighbourhood, with a view to break up the old *bazaár*. It is said of my millionaire that he thereupon went over personally to his own *bazaár*, and there accosted each dealer and fish-wife thus:

'You see I am an old man—a very old man. You are all my children. I have two children at home; but all the rest are here. Will you desert me, my children, in my old age? Has your father deserved this at your hands? If anything sits heavy on you, tell me of it and I will remove the oppression. Do you complain of anything—any misbehaviour on the part of my servants— any shortcomings of my own?'

They one and all said that they had no grievances to complain of; they one and all swore that they would never leave their old father's protection for all the new *bazaárs* that might be set up. Each dealer and fish-wife then received as presents, in ratification of the contract, a new cloth and sweetmeats. The rival *bazaár* had to shut up within a week.

Poor old man! He had perhaps no enemy in the world, and yet was not this man murdered? Of course I allude to the well-known Mádhub Dutt, who was killed on his way to his house at Chinsuráh from the railway station. The enigma of that story has not yet been explained. Justly or unjustly, suspicion looked askance in one particular direction; but no light whatever was thrown on the matter. It was supposed that one of his own *durwáns* was the selected agent for carrying out the crime, and this man, it is said, was afterwards traced to Lucknow, where he joined the mutineers and died sword in hand. But did that one man do the deed alone? Were there no accomplices? The mysteries of the Calcutta Police have yet to be unravelled.

The old man, as he came to me, had his *námamálá* in his hand, which he pattered as he chatted on. He was very happy, he said, at home. Of his two sons, the eldest had died some years ago; and that was his greatest grief. But Providence had toned down his sorrow. He spoke of his surviving son with the greatest affection. He loved to live at Chinsuráh, he said, because the place was so much quieter than Calcutta, and he wanted rest. Rumour had it that he was tied down to the spot by the silken meshes of an unorthodox love. Poor old man! Did he not pay too dearly for it? It was when going to this lady-love that he was waylaid and murdered. By whom? Will that ever transpire? Years have passed over the crime. Is it yet to the profit of any man to leave the tale untold?

CHAPTER XXVII. CALIGRAPHY—ITS DECLINE

A Deputy Magistrate, flaunting a gold chain, introduces himself. An old copyist—a wag of the first water—is looking admiringly at the chain, with great affected simplicity. The Deputy Magistrate is much flattered, and asks condescendingly if the old man likes the chain.

'Oh! it is not that, sir! The chain is good enough; and the gold is very bright too. But I am looking at it so steadfastly because it explains the meaning of a word which I never understood before.'

'What word can it be, I wonder?'

'Oh! a very simple word, sir; or rather two words. At home, my youngsters, in conning over their spelling-book, constantly repeat the words,—"a he-goat," "a she-goat."'

'Well, how do these words concern my chain?'

'Why, sir,' asks the old man with the greatest simplicity in the world, 'is not this a he-gote, and a she-gote too? Does it not answer as a *gote* (chain) both for yourself and your lady?'

The Deputy Magistrate was furious,—the copyist had run off.

The *keráni* referred to was a particularly impudent one, and presumed much on his age; but he was also very useful. He was both copyist and draftsman. A paper once came down to the office written in Arabic, which no one could read. Copies of the document were urgently wanted for circulation to Mofussil officers. This copyist, without understanding a single word of the language, made copies of the paper so exact that, when they were submitted to competent examiners for verification, not a single mistake was found in them. To do this, perhaps, did not require much intelligence; but it certainly did require great precision of hand to copy stroke for stroke, without mistaking a single twist.

Of one assistant of the office—an East-Indian—it was said that a certain Governor-General, who wrote a very crabbed hand, having asked for a copyist who should be able to copy every letter correctly without being able to understand a single word, this man was selected, and did his work to his Excellency's satisfaction. For this qualification he drew a specially large salary, and when on a later day it was proposed to curtail the amount, he strongly protested against any reduction, urging clamorously that, though he did not understand much of accounts, he was the only assistant in the office who could copy correctly without understanding the text! The plea was admitted, and the salary spared!

Some of the old copyists wrote an excellent hand. In this respect the falling off in later times has become very apparent. The old letters of the office were always written in splendid characters; but now-a-days the pot-hooks are scarcely readable. This is observable also in other documents. Just look at an old Government Promissory Note, or, as it is now the fashion to call those papers, an old 'Government *Security*.' The writing on it looks like copper-plate; but the Promissory Notes of the present day have nothing like it to show. Even the signatures of the officers in past days—those of Messrs. Prinsep, Bushby, and Morley, for instance—were very clear and legible; while the signatures of the present time can scarcely be deciphered without a competitive reading examination among half-a-dozen men; and yet the papers in those days used to be signed by the highest officers of the Government, who did not consider it beneath their dignity to write a clear hand; while now the papers are signed by mere Treasury clerks, who think it a shame to be able to write at all. I think that, like some millionaires I have mentioned, these gentlemen might simply put their mark on the papers with a x cross, and some subordinate assistant might then write underneath 'Mr. So-and-so'—'his mark.'

Then the old records of the Government offices, how beautifully they were kept! The same virtue of splendid handwriting is observable throughout them all. They are, page after page, quire after quire, ream after ream, unmarked by a blot or an erasure, and are always easily read without any pain to the eye. Printing has come to the rescue of the present generation, and all the printed records of every public office are of course very decent; but such records as happen to be kept in manuscript, how shabby they are! And yet the copyists of the present day are paid more, much more, liberally than were those of the past.

CHAPTER XXVIII. PATRONAGE—HOW VACANCIES IN GOVERNMENT OFFICES ARE FILLED UP

A nice appointment—that is, for an uncovenanted officer—has become vacant. There are many candidates for it—one among them *par excellence* the best of the whole lot, being a man of education, station in society, and much official experience. Another candidate is a very young man, of no official aptitude whatever, but very well connected, and personally known to Sir Henry Hardinge[14], with whose daughter he has danced in England! Will you bet who wins the prize? The man of parts was sanguine, but did not get it.

Take another case. A new appointment is created in an office where proverbially there is little work to do. The pay is handsome, and there are three candidates, two of whom would have graced any appointment. The third is illiterate, but has been of great service in divers unofficial ways (*e.g.* in procuring loans of money and the like) to the officer who has the nomination in his hands. The merits of all the candidates are well known. The great man's nominee gets the post; the fact being that it was created for him, with especially fat pay and no work, the admission of other candidates being all a sham.

The reader may say that this has been so from the commencement, and will be so to the end of time. Who knows of the golden age, when it was otherwise? True: but all this happens under the very nose of the Government; the nose gets the stink, and only tries to keep it off with 'kerchief and Eaude-Cologne; the eyes are conveniently closed, the saint seems absorbed in prayer, and the thing is done. It would be a different matter if the Government were altogether ignorant of these doings; but can it conscientiously plead that it is so?

A third instance refers to an humbler appointment. An assistant applies for a vacancy in a higher grade. There are other applicants also, but he has long been recognised as the best of the lot. He goes to the head of the office for it, and is refused; the claims of one of the other candidates being preferred.

'Very good, sir! But I have always had the toughest job to do, while the party preferred has had comparatively lighter and easier work; you have yourself said so on several occasions.'

'Yes, you are right; I have said so.'

'Then I trust, sir, this will be mended now. Since he gets the promotion, it will be only fair to give him the more important duties.'

'Oh! that's my look-out, not yours. I always apportion work according to the capabilities of my assistants. The question of pay has nothing to do with that.'

It is useless multiplying instances. No deserving man in the public service can look above him without seeing many inferior people hoisted far beyond his reach. He may feel aggrieved, but must expect no redress. He may wince; the withers of those in power are unwrung. One thing, however, he can do to regain his peace of mind. After looking up the ladder, he has only to look down; and if his mind be at all well regulated, he will at once see that there are many his equals, if not betters, occupying posts much lower than his own. The justice or the injustice of the thing need not be considered; it is not open for discussion or deliberation. There is the fact staring us in the face, and we must accommodate ourselves to it in the best way we can. Mr. So-and-so has got ahead of me most unjustly. Admitted; but similarly, you have got ahead of Báboos So-and-so, without possessing any higher merits. The beam will never get steady; the scales are constantly vacillating.

CHAPTER XXIX. THE NEW REGISTRAR

The old Registrar Sáheb has gone out, and a new Registrar Sáheb has come in. Is he a better man? No; certainly not better in respect to work, and infinitely worse in all other respects. Were there no better candidates to select from? Lots of them; but it is needless trying to discover the why and wherefore of such *contretemps*. A new broom must sweep. But he does not know what to sweep; so he sweeps away right and left, disorganizing everything, without understanding what he does disorganize. Many alterations are made by him—all slap-dash, without judgment or forethought. The most valuable cheques are vetoed and prohibited—new ones are ordered which answer no useful purpose. A flaming account is sent up to the Chief Accountant of the improvements carried out; and the zealous broom is thanked in set phrase for having rescued the office from chaos and confusion. The whole world is a clap-trap, my masters, and we ourselves are the players in it!

Now, who is this new Registrar? A very busy and energetic man he is, whose pretensions include all sorts of accomplishments, without real claim to any. He has dabbled in Greek and Latin, and is master of English, Scotch, Welsh, and Irish. Persian he pretends to; Arabic and Chinese he promises to learn. He sings scraps of bawdy songs to exhibit his knowledge of poetry; mouths and gesticulates, and strikes the table very hard with his fists to show that he is an orator; and pretends to have taken lessons from my deceased friend, Rádhá Náth Sikdár, out of Laplace and Newton.[15] It is sham throughout from top to bottom, and yet it is curious how men of education fail to detect the imposition. The man came out to this country with a wooden ladle in his mouth; entered some flourishing concern in the very humblest capacity; got on well enough there; pretended to have mastered the business; played his cards with great cleverness; and behold his wooden ladle is converted into a silver spoon—or you may call it golden without exaggeration.

'I will put you in the way; I will do everything for you,' mutters the deputy to his head, in the vain hope of ingratiating himself in his good graces.

'All right!' says the head, and makes over all his work to the deputy, and himself goes about gadding—to great people, to small people, and where not?

He remained in office long, very long indeed; and if he had only taken the pains to learn his work, he would have been worth something. But this he never did. He talked big, crowed loud, slapped the table hard, stamped with his feet, and cursed and swore by Sodom and Gomorrah. The *peons* and *duftries* of the office quaked at these energetic demonstrations; even *keránis* of the lower grades got funky, while those whom his arm could not reach laughed at him; and yet this man had long, very long, the reputation of being a very efficient Registrar—a man who did not know anything of work, and whose whole secret of administration was brow-beating.

The deputy who assisted him soon found out his mistake. He had angled very adroitly for favour, but never secured it. He got disappointed and less zealous; the head got disgusted and aweary, and the deputy was thrown overboard without the slightest compunction. But who was to do the work now?—such mechanical duties as did devolve on a Registrar and could not be slurred over? He got a *dewán* Báboo to do it—a member of that caste which, rightly or wrongly, has the credit of being the most intriguing and mischievous. The fellow acted both as deputy and spy; they say that he did even worse, but of that I have no certain information. It is in this way that most people get on in life. Fools, and those who can't help it, work; knaves get their work done by others, and simply draw their pay.

CHAPTER XXX. DEMOCRACY AND SEDITION

A Military Officer held his office in the same building with the Account Department, and, as he had plenty of leisure, he took a delight in coming over and breaking a lance with me as often as he could find time for it. The manner in which we became first acquainted was rather unpleasant. He had taken a fancy to the small room which I occupied, had asked for it from our Burrá Sáheb, and came to turn me out.

'Well, Báboo, how long have you occupied this room?'

'Nearly a year now.'

'But that has not given you any vested right to it, you know.'

'Certainly not; do you want it?'

'Very much indeed; and what is more, Mr.— has told me to take it. So it all depends upon you whether you will give it up or not.'

'I would have given it up to you even if Mr.— had not ordered it. I shall move out at once now, since he has told you to take it.'

'Oh no! there is no particular hurry about it. You can move out when you like. I was obliged to speak to Mr.—, because hitherto the room had belonged to his part of the office.'

The acquaintance thus commenced he took great pains to cultivate; and in all the banter and provoking discussions we had, I always found him a perfect gentleman. He one day came and asked me what my duties were, and tried to understand them, and then wanted to know what salary I received. All his inquiries having been answered, he coolly asked if I was not overpaid.

'Don't you think Rs.— too much for your duties?'

'Possibly, yes; taken in the abstract, the sum is large enough. But when I find that you are paid Rs.—, it then occurs to me for the first time that I am very much underpaid. Our duties are nearly similar; you have the military accounts, while I have those of the civil departments; and yet you get just eight times more than I do. Don't you think that to be somewhat unjust?'

The flush on his face was perceptible, but he covered it with a smile.

'I can got out a man from England,' he said, 'who would do your work for your pay.'

'I have not the slightest doubt of it,' said I; 'but that would give no saving to the Government. I can nominate a native who will do your work for a fourth of your salary, or if the Government insists on having a European, I can at any moment pick out from the unofficial ranks a countryman of your own, who will fill your chair as efficiently at least as you do for half the amount you draw.' This was a settler, and he ever after called me a democrat.

He came back to the charge when the papers announced the death of the Advocate-General, Mr. Ritchie. 'Can you give us a native who would fill up Mr. Ritchie's place?'

'No! I don't know any native, or any European civilian, or military officer either, who could take up his duties.'

'So you see your country can't give us the men we want, and we must get out fit men from England.'

'Just so, and my country is willing to pay handsomely for any available talent that England can lend her. What she complains of is that she has to feed so many drones[16] too in the bargain.'

'Meaning me and the like of me, I suppose?'

'Not particularly; but there may be parties whom the cap will fit.'

'But you forget that we have conquered the country, and are entitled to everything in it as a matter of course.'

'Possibly; but the country was lost by the Mahomedans, who had no inherent right to it. You did not fight the Hindus, and I contend that the Hindus have not forfeited their birthright.'

'Ho! ho! Are you prepared to fight out for your birthright now?'

'Perhaps to say so would be treason; but when I hear every individual Englishman arrogating to himself the conqueror's right, and bragging of it, I am almost tempted to have a play at quarter-staff with him, if only to convince him that each Englishman individually is not necessarily a conqueror.'

'We don't fight with quarter-staffs; we fight with guns and swords, which you don't know how to handle.'

'Only because you have schools to teach their use to you; but an enlightened Government has not thought fit to set up such schools in this country yet.'

'But if you had the schools, do you think there would be many volunteers to learn the art of fighting?'

'I can't answer that question exactly now, but I should say that there ought to be many pupils. The English are protecting us with great kindness, but many people may nevertheless wish to learn to protect themselves. The occasion may arise when it would be of inestimable value to them.'

'What occasion? Can you think of any?'

'Yes; England may get tired of the work of evangelizing India, and may give her up altogether some day when we least expect it, and then we are done for, only because the Government will not allow us to learn the use of arms.'

'Oh! you need not fear that England will give up India in a hurry.'

'Then there is the possibility of her being compelled to do so.'

'Indeed! All of you natives seem to think that Russia can take India at any moment from us; don't you?'

'I don't. I can't answer for others, but I don't believe that either Russia, or France, or America, or any other nation whatever, can snatch India from England alone. One to one England is quite a match, and probably more than a match, for the strongest of them. But there may be a coalition against her, and then, with two or three strong powers opposed to her, no alternative would, perhaps, remain to her but to give up India.'

'There is a deal of sense in what you say, but the purse of England is so long that of all powers in the world she has the least to fear from coalitions. No coalition against her could stand for six months; so you can rest quite satisfied that the protection of England will not be withdrawn from you. Is there any other reason why you want to have a military school?'

'Yes; the reasons for it are as plentiful as wild flowers. A military school would enable us to stand by and be of help to the English in the hour of need.'

'Or to join the rebels in the event of another mutiny? Eh!'

'You don't pay a compliment to Bengal. Bengal is too wide-awake for such folly.'

CHAPTER XXXI. ABOUT FARMING AND THE MUTINY

'I wonder,' said the Colonel, 'that, with such notions as you entertain, you came to serve the Government in such capacity as that of a *Keráni*.'

'What else could I do? Englishmen do not seem to see that the field for selection for us is a very circumscribed one.'

'Why, there are the professions open to you as to everybody else— Medicine, and the Bar.'

'The higher grades in both are not quite open to us; or rather require a visit to England, which is not very convenient to everybody.'

'Cultivation? Farming?'

'Yes; farming would pay handsomely. The thing is not understood in the country now, and if it were carried on fairly could not fail to be very remunerative. But you know the native objection to cattle-farming; we can't rear to kill.'

'Fudge! nonsense! Why, my friend, at every *Poojáh*—excuse me that I use strong words—you kill most brutally and unnecessarily hundreds and thousands of cattle as hecatombs; and after that can you possibly feel any real compunction in slaughtering animals for the sustenance of human life?'

'You argue very strongly indeed. I cannot justify the prejudice; but, like many other anomalies, it does exist, and therefore is cattle-farming impracticable for an orthodox Hindu.'

'But you are not an orthodox Hindu, surely?'

'My seniors are, and I am bound to respect their feelings in the matter. Besides, if I did establish a good farm, would I not have many troubles along with it? Your indigo-planters have the bad name of making free with the crops of other people whenever they find it of advantage to them to act in that way. Will not European cattle-farmers of the same stamp rise up and try their hand at cattle-lifting on a wholesale scale?'

'Try their hand at cattle-lifting! Why, man, you threatened me with the quarter-staff the other day. Could you not make that ring in earnest on the head of a rival cattle-farmer? That is the way the Dandie Dinmonts settle such differences in my native land, and you must do likewise.'

'Just so, and be perpetually in hot water, and perpetually bribing the *ámláhs* of the law courts. The work would doubtless be very remunerative, but perhaps not very pleasant.'

'You should go and live in Utopia then, if you want everything to be made very pleasant for you.'

'I should indeed; only I don't know whereabouts it lies.'

A very good man was the Colonel. He liked to provoke me to speak freely with him, and never betrayed the slightest impatience when I retorted; but on many subjects we thought alike. An assistant of the Account Office had accompanied Peel's brigade[17] against the mutineers as a police-officer, I think. He brought back with him various articles as booty, such as gold and silver ornaments, silver-plate, shawls, brocades, velvet *chádurs* worked with gold, and the like. He held a market of them in the office, and many were the purchasers. I did not buy anything. This was observed, and the Colonel, who came in, asked why.

'I don't know, sir, how these things have been come by.'

'Why, they have been taken from the mutineers red-handed, I suppose.'

'Or possibly from people who were called mutineers that they might be plundered?'

'Now, now, that is very uncharitable, surely. Do you think that a party of Englishmen, with an educated, kind-hearted English officer at their head, could be guilty of such a dereliction of duty as that?'

'Well, I don't know what to say. The English officers in cold blood would do nothing so brutally unjust, I know; but they are demons when their blood is up, and this the mutiny has proved incontestably everywhere. People have been hanged and shot to death who were no more mutineers than you or I, and whose only misfortune was that they came across the avenging parties by accident. Just look here, Colonel; here is a nose-ring, an ornament used only by females. Do you mean to say that there were females fighting among the mutineers?'

'No; but the trinket was doubtless found among property belonging to the mutineers; how come by they knew best.'

'Or may be it was torn off by the avenging army from the nose of some poor woman who did not know where to fly for protection.'

'Ah! you are a poet, with a fine, vigorous imagination, and will doubtless give us your version of the mutinies in an epic by and by.'

'Full of stories more dreadful than those told by Ugolino?[18] No; the governors would not like anything of that sort coming from the governed. I should be set down as a mutineer myself if I attempted it. We must leave it to Englishmen to tell the story for us, and my confidence in Englishmen is so great that I have no doubt that, sooner or later, the tale will be most faithfully told.'

'I thank you indeed for the compliment,' said the Colonel; 'you are the most queer native that I have known.'

Chapter XXXII. Beggars on Horseback

Set a beggar on horseback and he will ride to the d—l, says the adage. True; but then who is to blame that he does ride so? Not the beggar surely, but he who places him on horseback.

There was such a beggar in our office—an Englishman of exceedingly rough manners. His antecedents are not known to me. He had been a schoolmaster, and was picked up for the office on being turned out from the school, under the impression that a pedagogue must necessarily be a dab at figures. They made much of him because he was English-born, though in reality his stupidity was as dense as granite. Besides this density he had some other recommendations. His partiality to the bottle once brought him into a serious scrape. He had been summoned to attend the High Court as a juror, and had there committed a nuisance—the cat may as well be let out of the bag—he had * * * * * * in the jury-box. The Judge was furious; but after a severe lecture he contented himself by imposing a fine of Rs. 50, if I remember aright. This was the man, sirs, who found favour with an Accountant imported from the deserts of Cobi; and they made him—well, never mind what they made him; they placed him on horseback.

He was an altered man at once. No one who spoke to him without a preface of three *saláms* was ever looked at. He issued orders after orders like the Czar of Russia, and the assistants subordinate to him had to codify these, and append to them an alphabetical index for prompt reference. Written replies to his questions not submissively worded were returned as incomplete and impertinent; verbal replies were arrogant if not interlarded with the word 'sir' after every five words. One day an assistant *not* subordinate to him was going down the staircase when he was coming up. The assistant, though a nigger and on small pay, had made no *salám*.

'You there, why don't you make your *salám* to me? Do you know who I am?'

'Yes, I know you very well; but there is no *saláming* order in force in this office.'

'Will you make your *salám* to me, or not?'

'I shall consider and let you know.'

'Will you make your *salám* now, on the spot?'

'No, I won't.'

'Very well, sir; that will do.'

The eyes threatened; but the threat did not fructify. Perhaps the gentleman from Cobi who had placed the beggar on horseback was ashamed to back him in such a ridiculous squabble; and so the matter dropped.

Scenes equally ridiculous are acted almost every day in all the Government offices generally, there being no lack of indigent equestrians in any of them. One fellow, an East-Indian, but placed in authority, enters a room where he finds a poor clerk, who has just come to office quite weary, seated on his chair. The clerk had not risen from his seat; why should he? he is occupying his own seat, and is doing, or is about to commence, his own work.

'Why don't you rise from your seat when I come in?'

What is the man to do? His position does not allow him to ask in return, why he should? He is therefore obliged to render the homage required of him.

I remember having once witnessed a different scene, which I record here with pleasure. A native assistant used to wait in the portico every day till the head of the department, a European, came to office, when he would make him three humble *saláms* and then go about his work. This went on for some days without any remark. At last the great man could hold out no longer. He sent for the assistant into his own room, and asked him why he *salámed* to him in that manner every day. 'Either you take me for an ass whom you fancy you can easily buy over by your meanness, in which case you are a knave; or you are an ass yourself and do not know what you are about. Now take care that I do not catch you at this trick again; for if I do, I will degrade you.'

Another scene of a different sort may also come in here for want of a better place to put it in. One European Registrar was a little deaf, and used always to place his open hand behind the ear when listening to anything attentively. A native assistant took it into his head to imitate him in this, possibly expecting that that would please the great man. He found out his mistake soon.

'God d—n you, sir,' exclaimed the pious Registrar; 'why do you put up your hand in that way? I do it because I am deaf; you are not deaf, you blockhead.'

CHAPTER XXXIII. THIS PICTURE AND THAT

I have depicted some drunkards before. I shall here give the life of another representative specimen of the class. Judoo was the son of a poor widow, and was known from his earliest days as a very nice young man. Fathers singled him out as a model for their children to imitate. 'He has nobody to look after him, yet see what a good boy he is reckoned at school. If you can only be like him, I would be fully satisfied.' Such, or similar, were often the confidential exhortations of many a parent to his son. This young man, the pride of his mother, in whom all the affections of her widowed heart were centred, left school with credit, got into a Government office, and for a long time pursued a steady and exemplary life. Promotion follows steadiness—at least often, if not always; and Judoo got on pretty well in life—very well indeed for one of such poor parentage. Unfortunately he got into an office in which there were pickings to get besides pay, and these fluctuating additions to his income undid him. The d—l's fee does not come in for nothing. It was something distinct from his salary, and did not find a place in his regular accounts. How was the money to be spent? He was no longer a young man now; the heyday of life had already gone by: but the man who had been strict in his morals in his youth, now that he was the father of several children, was not ashamed to frequent the shops of infamy. One crime brought with it another; the company he had chosen could only be endured under the fumes of brandy or usquebaugh; the bottle therefore stepped forward where it was so absolutely needed.

And now he found his perquisites too small to keep pace with his habits. There was first his light-o'-love to maintain; and next a supply of spirits and necessary accompaniments to be found every night for self, her, and such others, her friends, as she chose to bring in. The pickings in the office could not cover all this expenditure. The comforts hitherto allowed to wife and children began therefore to be curtailed. But still ways and means did not square; debts began to accumulate, and the interest that had to be paid for them only made the difficulty still greater; the consumption of liquid fire began also to increase, and at last the office accounts were tampered with, which upon discovery was visited with dismissal.

Income and pickings both gone, how was this man now to live? The widow-mother died broken-hearted; the wife from comparative comfort descended to wretchedness; the children were utterly neglected, and grew up corrupt almost from their youth; while their father dangled after the rich, helping them in their vices, and living on their charity. Was brandy given up? No. One son was killed in a brawl in an empty-house; another convicted of burglary and imprisoned. Fearful was the visitation of the Most High! Do we always read them aright?

As a counterpart to this picture I shall give that of another widow's son, who started life under still poorer circumstances. Yes, this widow was very poor indeed; she went from house to house in her neighbourhood to collect for her son, perhaps for herself also, the leavings of rice and curry in the kitchen; and also for torn clothes and torn shoes! Her son received no education—absolutely none; all her exertions were barely able to keep body and soul together; and when he had become a big lubberly boy, he entered the engineering school. Very little scholastic attainments were required in those days for the study he selected; he learnt his profession well. Even at that time he was propped up by the collections of food and clothing made by his mother from house to house. On one occasion she came to me with a most woeful countenance to say that her son must go to school barefooted unless I could give her a pair of old shoes. He is now an assistant-engineer, I believe, and contemplates giving to the appointment, to open out a professional career for himself independent of state support.

Take another instance. A young widow with two children, a boy and a girl, came to Calcutta from the mofussil to see what could be done for them. She took service with a rich family as a menial-servant, worked with extra zeal to win favour, and succeeded. Her boy was taken in hand by the head of the family, and received an education along with his own children. He benefited by it sufficiently to be able to retain a good appointment which his patron's exertions obtained for him, and was in time able to secure a fortune and position for himself.

These instances are not ideal. In the first case the bottle seared up all the promises of early life. In the second and the third, the opening prospects were not half so hopeful as in the first; but Áhriman was not allowed admittance, and the design of Áhoormazd[19] bore fruit.

CHAPTER XXXIV. THE LAST

As an assistant in favour, I had occasionally to dance attendance on the higher covenanted officers of the department at their private residences, and this gave me an opportunity to observe their modes of living attentively. It is well known that they all live in grand style when their families are with them; but I observed that when the Mem Sáheb was away they lived very poorly indeed. Of one gentleman the sleeping cot was more wretched than the one I use, nor had he more than half-a-dozen chairs in his house, the whole furniture of which was as ricketty as could well be conceived. Nor was his an isolated instance. Altogether, it seems to me that the native mode of living is, on the whole, not less expensive than the English mode *minus* Mem Sáheb's expenses on finery, education of the children in England, and the cost of wines. The beef and the *moorgee* may cost a trifle more than fish and vegetables; but the waste of cooked food in native families is something awful, as each member is served separately, and what remains on the platter of one cannot be transferred to that of another, nor taken back into the kitchen. Perhaps not less than one-fourth of the food cooked comes thus to be thrown away. The cost of clothing would probably on both sides be also found to be equal, or nearly so. It is true that the Báboo goes about half-naked. But his shawls, and *pugrees*, and *kincobs* cost a deal more than the shirts and coats of Mr. Brown; and, even including Mem Sáheb's finery, the gold and silver trinkets of Gokool Moni run up the expenses of Rám Bose to a very heavy amount. Of course old Brown has to pay a large sum of money for house-rent, while Rám Dádá occupies the little fort his ancestors built a few years after the flood, on which he has never laid out more than twenty rupees a year in repairs. But the original outlay on Castle Dangerous must have been pretty considerable, and the interest on that money, if it does not quite come up to the monthly disbursement of Brown, is still a good set-off against it. Brown's expenditure on wines must be considerable, against which Rám Churn, if orthodox, has nothing to show beyond the eight annas a month he pays for his tobacco; but his hopeful, Mr. Bose, promises to run up the account under this head in a short time; and then the accounts will probably be squared on both sides, provided the present practice of Rám Bose, Siboo Bose, and Hurro Bose congregating together under the same roof, is simultaneously abandoned. The go-a-head generation is fighting hard for an equality, and will have it—in respect to expenses at least. They already call their thrifty fathers 'pigs,' classing themselves doubtless under the head of 'monkeys.' The pig has the reputation of being a stupid animal, and the monkey that of a devilish clever one; but naturalists will observe that species vary.

I have spun out these reminiscences much longer than I intended. A contribution of this nature can, of course, be protracted to any length; but I am very averse to take advantage of that circumstance. Enough, says the adage, is *as good* as a feast; my comment on the text is that enough is *better* than a feast, and, as the reader has had enough of my notes and lectures, our parting for the present is well-timed.

Shunkur: A Tale of the Indian Mutiny of 1857

[By Shoshee Chunder Dutt. From *Bengaliana: A dish of Rice and Curry, and Other Indigestible Ingredients.*]

CHAPTER I. THE CONSPIRATORS

The whole of India is more or less studded with temples and sacred edifices, some of which are beautifully situated either in the midst of thick groves or on the rugged summit of dark mountains, to which numerous pilgrims from all parts of the country come loaded with offerings, in all seasons of the year. An antique building of this description, not utterly destitute of architectural elegance and proportion, was to be seen some twenty years ago on the banks of the Ganges, at about an equal distance between Bithoor and Cáwnpore, surrounded on three sides by gardens of singular beauty, while the river washed its base on the fourth. The building was of a very chaste design, and was dedicated to the worship of Mahádeva or Arghanáth, whose image in black stone was cherished within it. The grounds around were extensive, and sprinkled with groves of banian-trees, which concealed from observation numerous other edifices appertaining to the temple, and also gave shelter to hosts of pilgrims from the noonday heat. The *mohunt,* or *sabáit* of the god, was an old man, who had counted more than sixty summers, but still retained a tall and upright form. His head and beard were grey, but his eyes were bright and piercing almost as those of youth, and gave fearful significance to a countenance that was peculiarly ill-boding. But the man had, nevertheless, a great reputation for sanctity, and the rich men of the neighbourhood vied with each other in showing him respect.

In India the hot season commences with March. It was on the eve of a rather sultry day of that month, in the year of Christ 1857, that two men were to be seen sauntering near the precincts of the temple, under the banian-groves, almost in moody silence, or occasionally exchanging a few words with each other, as if afraid to speak out their minds more freely. One of them was the priest we have described; the other was a younger middle-sized man, with a stout frame, a round pock-marked face, and very intelligent but ill-expressioned eyes. He was dressed more like an English gentleman than a Hindu, in tight trousers and a brocaded caftan, while he flourished an ivory-mounted sword-stick in his hand. The evening was very tranquil; the sun had recently set, and already a beautiful moon, such as is only to be seen in the tropics, was in the sky, piercing through the sombre shadow of the trees, and flooding the broad breast of the river below with her soft and silver radiance. The spot and the hour were in fact well-suited for the purpose which had brought the two men together; and they were impatiently waiting for the arrival of others whom they expected, and a frown was already gathering on the face of the younger man at their delay.

'Our friends are laggards, and it is not safe to have loiterers to deal with in such affairs,' said the younger man.

'You have reached the place of assignation sooner, prince, than was agreed upon,' quietly expostulated the priest.

'What then? Should they not have come here earlier than me? But I am unreasonable. What company have you got in the temple to while away the time?'

'If you mean girls, we have none there to-night. But I can send for the barber's pretty wife who pleased you so much, if you want her.'

'Pooh! the lion does not feast on the same carcass twice; if you want to please me you must get me a new mistress every time.'

'There will be no difficulty in that, I assure you. But, prince, your orders for privacy to-night were strict, and no arrangements of the kind have therefore been made.'

'You are right, Thákoorjee. There is no time for love-making now; and I think our laggards have arrived at last.'

Some heavy steps and the rustling of fallen leaves showed that the conjecture of the prince was correct, and immediately after two figures emerged from the trees that were nearest, and stood before them. The first of these was a slim young man, of a dark olive complexion and rather prepossessing appearance, dressed after the manner of the East, with much finery and gold. The other was a stout, thickset man of about fifty, having more the appearance of a Cossack of the Ukraine than of a native of Hindustán; dressed like a respectable Mahomedan, but exhibiting an appearance decidedly unprepossessing, of which the most prominent features were high cheek-bones, small restless eyes, and a frame indicative in all parts of great personal strength.

We may as well introduce to the reader the several characters before him. The prince was no other than Náná Dhoondoopunt, *alias* Náná Sáheb, the notorious hero of the Cáwnpore atrocity, a man of great intelligence, who could read and write English, and who lived like an English gentleman, a good deal by the cover side. He was the adopted son of Bájee Ráo, ex-Peishwá of Pooná, and his grievance against the British Government was that the pension of £80,000 paid to the Peishwá, was not continued to him. His means were ample, all the private wealth of the Peishwá having been inherited by him; and he lived in the Peishwá's castle at Bithoor, just ten miles west of Cáwnpore, having a personal retinue of two hundred armed men, with three guns, quite independent of British authority. The priest of the temple was Náná's pimp, astrologer, and confidanté [sic]. The young Mahomedan was Ázimooláh Khán, who represented the Mahomedan interests in the councils of Bithoor, had proceeded to the Crimea, during the Russian War, to see with his own eyes the relative strength of England, France, and Russia, and had come back impressed with a very unfavourable opinion of English pluck and energy. The heavier Mussulman pretended to represent some foreign power,[20] though he was accredited by none; but it was his advice and directions that gave a plan and system to the Sepoy revolt of 1857.

CHAPTER II. THEIR LAST CONFERENCE

The evening was deepening into night when the conspirators sat down at their place of rendezvous, under the shadow of the banian-trees.

'I have not failed you, prince,' said the thickset Mussulman, opening the conference.

'I am glad you have not,' said Náná. 'We must come to some definite understanding without further delay.'

'Yes; we have lost considerable time already, but it was not my fault. I understood that both you and the Khán Báhádoor had proceeded on a pilgrimage, and were absent from the country.'

'A very holy pilgrimage it was on which we went—a Mahomedan and a Hindu together! You are dying to know all about it. We visited all the military stations along the Grand Trunk Road as far as Umbállá, to gauge the feelings of the troops located in those places.'

'And what was the result?'

'Ask the Khán Báhádoor; he will tell you,' said the Náná, looking sulky and overcast.

Ázimoolláh, who was thus appealed to, seemed indisposed to give any direct reply, and at last only said that the prospects were not very pleasing, but that he still hoped for the best.

'Nay, speak out, Ázimoolláh,'said Náná, 'and tell the blunt truth at once. You need not fear to hurt my feelings. I wish you joy and success in your career; but if they won't have me, why I can seek my fortune alone.'

'Bless me, if I understand a word of all this!' observed the Mussulman who had opened the conference. 'Who will not have you? Who are the parties who can do without you?'

Náná replied not, while Ázimooláh Khán looked embarrassed, and turned uneasily on his seat; but the priest now broke silence, and stated how the case stood. The troops at every station had refused to make Náná their leader. Even those at Cáwnpore, among whom he had spent large sums of money, would not rise except for the old king of Delhi.

'That is all a mere excuse, you know,' said Náná. 'The men have no stomach for the big work we proposed to them. They are afraid of that rotten power of which the English brag so much.'

After this there was a long pause in the conversation, which was at last broken by the thickset Mussulman.

'Ever since I came to this country,' said he, 'I have made many inquiries far and wide in respect to the feelings of the army, and my conviction always has been that their disaffection to the Government is very general. The discipline of the army is lax. All the sepoys complain everywhere of unnecessary restrictions imposed upon them. The arrogance of the young officers is represented as insufferable, The subadár-major who has fought twenty battles is treated contemptuously and spoken of as a "nigger" by the young lieutenant who has barely learnt to flaunt his epaulettes before the ladies. The slowness of promotion is everywhere complained of, and also the limited nature of the rewards open to the really good soldier. The army, in fact, is thoroughly disorganized; the little consideration shown for the feelings and caste-prejudices of the men has spread disaffection everywhere; and I cannot but believe that the troops in every place are quite ripe for a revolt, and would rise up to a man under a proper leader.'

'And who should that leader be?' broke out Náná in great petulance. 'The attenuated old man of Delhi, or the bastard of Lucknow? For whom must Náná of Bithoor, the son of Bájee Ráo, make way? Point out a worthy man to replace me, and I recede at once. But ask me not to fight for a boy of fourteen, whose mother goes nightly to bed with a paramour; or for a diminutive old dolt whom another boy calls father, while his mother undisguisedly attempts daily to fly out of the palace, and speaks of her husband as a nasty cross old man, with whom she is heartily disgusted.'

'But we don't ask you to fight for either, prince, but only for yourself,' said Ázimooláh. 'The pith of the matter is easily understood. The sepoys will not rally except around the old king. Why should we not make use of his name to bring them out? I, though a Mahomedan, am not very enthusiastic in the cause either of Jummá Bukht or his father. The latter is too old to make a good king, and the character of the mother of Jummá Bukht will always leave his birth doubtful; besides which, he does not give any indications of future fitness. Huzrut Mul, the Begum of Oude, notwithstanding her passion for Mummoo Khán, I regard with admiration. I respect her courage and energy, and for her sake would befriend the cause of Birjis Kádder, her son. But my devotion to the Mahomedan interests will never blind me to the fact that there is only one man in all India, and that man a Hindu, worthy to become leader in this great emergency, and I make it no secret that my only wish is to bring to him all the support which the Mahomedans throughout the empire can afford.'

'You speak fair, Khán Báhádoor, and I believe you,' said Náná; 'but if the troops marshal only under the banner of the old king, they will surely proclaim him Emperor of all India after the fighting work is over.'

'And that much,' said Ázimooláh, 'you must concede to him. The Mahomedan rule immediately preceded that of the English, and must be restored; but the Hindu power was also dominant over a large part of India, which only owned nominal allegiance to the Moslem, and that power will rest in your hands. Is not that a cause worth fighting for?'

Náná was silent for a time, and then asked gently,—'Is that your scheme?'

'Yes,' said Ázimooláh, 'that is the scheme which the Mahomedans all over the country will support; namely, that the kingdom be divided, and one part of it be given up to the Hindus to rule over, and the other part taken possession of by the Mahomedans, the puppet at Delhi retaining a nominal supremacy over all. You have only to say now whether you will accept or reject this scheme.'

'And look you here, prince, into this map,' said the Mahomedan akin to a Cossack; 'it has been prepared by my master, and defines clearly the partition he proposes between the Mahomedans and the Hindus, to set all quarrels for the future at rest. All the land here marked green, from the Nermuddá river to Cape Comorin, will own the future Peishwá of India as its sovereign lord, who might only send some elephants annually to Delhi in token of amity and affection. All the land marked yellow, from Ágrá to Cáchár, will similarly belong to the sovereign of Lucknow, who will also acknowledge a nominal fealty to the throne of Delhi. The rest of the country, marked blue, which is the smallest portion of the three, will belong immediately to the Emperor of Delhi, who will, in addition to it, be recognised as the lord-paramount of all India.'

'The Mahomedan to be lord-paramount again!' murmured Náná Saheb sulkily, unwilling to reject the scheme wholly, and still averse to accept it as it stood.

'It was so before,' said Ázimooláh, 'and must be so now; but the dominions allotted to the Peishwá by the partition are larger than ever were owned by any Hindu sovereign in any age.'

There was a dead pause again, which no one seemed anxious to break. At last Nániá turned slowly to the Cossack-looking Mussulman, and said, 'You say your master has chalked out this partition for us. Does he guarantee our possession to each?'

'You know already that you have my master's cordial moral support in this matter. Material support he will not render till there is interference against you on the part of other foreign powers. The English you must fight alone, and pitch them back into the seas they came from. If any other power comes to their aid, or pounces on India, or on any portion of it, after them, my master will support your cause heartily with arms.'

'I understand. He will assist us when we don't want his assistance,' returned Nániá, with a grim, sarcastic smile; but he changed his tone immediately after, and added, 'but perhaps your master means kindly, and it is ungracious to push back the hand that is loyally offered. We may require his aid hereafter, and he alone could aid us thoroughly against the Afgháns. Tell your master that I accept the partition he has made, and only do so because he has willed it. Otherwise Nániá Dhoondoopunt would have been at the bottom of the river below before he had conceded the lord-paramountship of India to a Mahomedan.'

So ended the last great conference of the conspirators before the mutiny broke out.

CHAPTER III. THE QUIET VILLAGE

The village of Soorájpore stood on the banks of the Ganges at a distance of about thirty miles from the city of Cáwnpore. It had nothing peculiar to distinguish it from other Indian villages of the same kind except this, that the huts in it were generally built with a reddish ferruginous clay, which gave them a cleaner appearance than huts built of dark mud present in other places. They were most of them thatched with bamboo and straw, though not a few were also to be found roofed with tiles. The village was altogether a poor one, the richest family having scarcely more than three or four huts, exclusive of a cooking-hut, a storehouse, and a cow-shed. Throughout the entire village there were only two houses built of brick, namely, one which belonged to a retired Subadár, and the other a small round temple dedicated to Káli, the wife of the Great Destroyer. The houses of the villagers were all contiguous, or nearly so, and the streets leading to them, though narrow, were for the most part straight and clean.

The month of May is a very hot month in India, when the winds breathe fire, and cause both flowers and verdure to droop and wither. But it is nevertheless not without its enjoyments, and as a rule the Hindu is very partial to his festivals, and enjoys them heartily whenever they come round. One of the most brilliant *fêtes* of the season is that held on account of the *Dasahárá*, or *Gungá Poojáh*, which generally comes in about the end of the month, or at the commencement of June. The crowds that assemble on the occasion are immense throughout all the Gangetic provinces, and it is a rare sight to see them proceed to the river-side to offer their oblations to the goddess Gungá, and purify themselves in her sacred waters. The processions of women are particularly interesting. Most of the fair ones go loaded with ornaments; but their garments conceal everything—their own fair persons and the trinkets they wear;—and the eye only sees forms veiled like Grecian statues in their graceful drapery, toddling forward with each other's support, while the ear is charmed with the tinkling of their ornaments, mingled with their merry but suppressed laughter, and accents peculiarly soft and sweet.

It was a galá-day in the little village of Soorájpore, and the villagers enjoyed it with hearty good-will. The amusements were of diverse kinds, though not characterized by any great display of physical energy. There was plenty of singing and gossiping; and the usual diversions of a country-fair were not wanting. Many good people were also pleasing themselves by making what is elsewhere called 'an April fool' of each other in diverse ways; and gambling, the vice of half-cultivated minds in all countries, was being indulged in with patient tranquillity. Festivity, like grief, however, has also its end, and by the time the sun had declined in the west the Poojáh processions were all terminated, and the idlers in the streets were breaking up, and each man and woman going about his or her ordinary avocations.

At the door of one of the cleanest ranges of huts a half-naked lad of eight years was, at this time, playing and singing with the boisterous merriment of his age. He was a fine stout boy for his years, and beside him sat a modest matron of about five-and-twenty, evidently his mother, the general contour of whose figure gave indications that her pretensions to beauty were not inconsiderable. Very little of her person was to be seen, as the cloth she wore was wrapped two or three times round the body, one end of it being fastened to the waist, while the other passed over the head, shoulders, and bosom, and then fell in front almost as low as her feet. But a curious observer might still have detected glimpses of a fine luscious face, beautiful dark eyes, and well-tapered limbs, albeit the skin, though polished as velvet, was only dark-brown. Not very far from this matron was an older woman, of about five-and-fifty, whose general resemblance to her daughter was too great for their relationship to each other being mistaken. Both these females, who had completed the religious observances of the day earlier than others, were now busy with their household work—cleansing rice and pulse for their homely fare; and, intent on their own occupation, they scarcely observed the proceedings of laggard revellers in the street.

'No business to-day, no work of any kind. This is a holiday; enjoy it, lads and lasses, while it lasts,' bawled out one lusty fellow, who was imitating the gestures of a Yogi, and had smeared his face with ashes, and was scattering mud and dust all round at his comrades.

'Hush! hush! There comes a Sowár on a great horse; I wonder wherefore, and to what end?' observed another of the party.

'The man wears the uniform of the great Rájáh of Bithoor. What can be his errand in this quiet place of ours?' spoke a third with alarm.

All eyes were now directed towards the horseman, who, coming up to the group, halted abruptly, and asked if any one would give him shelter and rest in the village till the following morning. The request was received in silence and with surprise. Even at this time the name of Náná was always spoken of with fear for miles around Bithoor, and no one wished to harbour any of his retainers for the briefest period, though they were all afraid to say so. The equestrian was tall and well-shaped, but very old. He nevertheless retained his seat on horseback well, and seemed inured to all the privations of active service.

'Well, bumpkins,' said he, 'must I ask again whether any of you will house me?'

'You have not told us yet,' said one of the villagers, 'whence you come and whither you are bound.'

'That, my friend, is my business, not yours,' said the man proudly. 'You know from my dress and bearing that I follow the lead of the Rájáh of Bithoor. Will any of you, for his sake or mine, give me a night's shelter, for I ask no more?'

'Ah, sir! we are all very poor people here,' was the reply of the village spokesman; 'we have scarcely more than a hut for each family, and certainly no decent bed for a gentleman like you. If you will only pass on to the brick-built house there, which is called the Subadár's Castle, you will doubtless receive such reception as you are entitled to, and as we cannot afford.'

'Oh! as to that,' said the horseman, 'any manner of reception will do excellently well for me, and these clean huts before us will fit me better, I think, than any brick-built house where two old soldiers, the Subadár and I, may perhaps be wrangling before the space of an hour is over.'

It is not customary with Hindu females, even of the humbler ranks, to speak to strangers, and when the two women heard of the preference expressed by the equestrian for their huts they whispered to the boy, who represented the male part of the family, to say bluntly that, as the master of the house was not present, they could not possibly make room for a stranger in it.

'Ha! my young friend, an excellent moss-trooper will you make before many years are over. But wherefore do you reject me? Do I frighten you? See, I am an old man,' and he took off his *pugree* to exhibit his grey hairs. 'Neither you, nor your mother, nor your grandmother need be afraid of me; and a night's shelter to a retainer of Nánà Sáheb will secure you, my young man, such service in time as all your compeers here will envy.'

The women, however, would not agree to the arrangement proposed; and their neighbours interfered to urge that it was unusual and unseemly.

'Be it so, ladies; I was not about to make love to you: and if you good bumpkins here cannot house me somewhere amongst you all, I must, I suppose, press on to the Subadár's residence.'

And so it was eventually decided; for the villagers one and all declined the honour of accommodating a man so suspicious-looking as the old equestrian, whom the reader will perhaps have already recognised as the priest of Arghanáth, and the confidanté of Nánà Sáheb.

Chapter IV. At Cáwnpore

The emissary of Nánà Sáheb left Soorájpore early on the next morning, and during the whole of that day there was nothing to be heard in the village but surmises as to his errand and destiny. The old Subadár with whom he had lodged was glum, and nothing could be got out of him but hints of vague rumours being afloat that Queen Victoria had ordered the wholesale conversion of the natives of India,[21] by compelling the Mahomedans to feed on pork, and the Hindus on beef for one week. The greatest indignation was of course expressed on all sides that an order so outrageously arbitrary should have been issued; there were several who did not believe in it; but others who did gave out further that the army, which alone had refused to submit to it, had been already directed to be disarmed and disbanded: and the faith of these believers was fearfully confirmed by the news which reached the village in the evening, that the troops stationed at Meerut and Delhi had broken out in revolt.

'Has this really occurred?' was the inquiry on all sides.

'Hush! don't speak of it aloud,' said the old Subadár, 'but the news is true. The English troops in India have received peremptory orders to cram down beef and pork into the mouth of every native, whether in service or out of it, and all who resist are to be hanged or shot.'

The alarm was now general, though there were still some infidels who shook their heads in disbelief. 'The English Government,' these said, 'has never betrayed such despotic earnestness on behalf of its own creed before. Why should it do so now?' To quiet such doubts came in the prompt reply that the Queen of England had dreamed a dream, in which she had talked face to face with Áhriman, the author of evil, who had threatened her with grave threats if all her subjects were not given up to him through the impious rite of baptism that he had established. And the news spread like wildfire through the country, from village to village, from the fisherman's cottage to the *kothee* of the Tehsildár.

The news of the outbreak at Meerut and Delhi reached Cáwnpore on the 14th of May. At that time the European force at Cáwnpore consisted of fifty-nine artillerymen and six guns, fifteen men of the 1st Madras Fusiliers, sixty men of H. M.'s 84th Regiment, and seventy men of H. M.'s 32nd Invalids; while the native troops consisted of the 2nd Regiment of Light Cavalry, the 1st, 53rd, and 56th Regiments of Infantry, and the Golundáuzes, or native gunners, attached to the battery. Besides the European force, the European population in cantonment included many civil officers and merchants, almost the whole of the soldiers' wives of H. M.'s 32nd Regiment, and many children, the total number amounting to about seven hundred and fifty souls. Great fears were necessarily felt in respect to the feelings of the native soldiery on the spot, though all the officers believed that, even if the men did break out, no attempt would be made by them to hurt or molest the Europeans.

'Would they harm us, the brutes, if they rise?' asked Mrs. Quinn, in alarm.

'No,' said Mrs. Burney. 'The sepoy is not so bad as that, you know. The fact is I don't believe that our sepoys here will rise at all. Captain Green has perfect confidence in the loyalty and fidelity of his men, and heard with great pain the proposal to disarm them.'

'That's my idea, too,' said Mrs. Burke; 'and Private O'Connor was telling my husband that he saw many of the suspected men crying bitterly at the want of confidence shown towards them.'

'It is only the scoundrels of the *bazaar*, I suppose,' remarked Mrs. Hussy, 'that give out these idle reports. But our old brigadier is a brick, and is not likely to do anything in a funk.'

'And besides that,' said Mrs. Cullen, 'we have a firm and stanch friend in Náná Sáheb, who is the *de facto* ruler of these parts, you know; and he is a knight without reproach or shame. He would not allow us to be harmed, any more than he would suffer his old mother at Bithoor to be roasted.'

'Oh! if the old general would only send for Náná,' said Mrs. Macgrath, 'and ask him to look after the station, how very safe we would all feel amidst these disquieting doubts!'

Despite these expressions of hope and confidence, however, there was a general sense of depression all over the station. The European merchants and others even went so far as to provide themselves with boats and other means of escape, but afterwards abandoned the idea of deserting the place, on being assured that, even if there was an outbreak, all that the native troops would attempt to do would be to possess themselves of the money lodged in the treasury, and then march off to Delhi to join the sovereign who had been there proclaimed.

'Now don't be alarmed, my dear,' said Mr. Tape to his better-half; 'the general is preparing an entrenched camp for us all, and the commissioner is laying in a supply of *áttá, dál, ghee,* and rum, calculated to last for three months for a thousand souls, so that even if the black devils become really mischievous, they will find us fully prepared.' And so all determined to stay where they were. After this who shall refuse to believe in destiny?

CHAPTER V. AT BITHOOR

We hasten now to the castle of Bithoor, within which, in a lofty apartment adorned with a profusion of chandeliers and mirrors, sat on a high-raised velvet cushion a grand sphinx-faced old woman, of a calm, stern aspect, the putative mother of Náná, and queen-dowager of the Mahrattás, as the people of the castle called her. She sat alone, her broad, lofty brow furrowed and full of thoughts; she had a rosary in her hand, and was turning the beads listlessly.

A light step approached the apartment; it was that of a beautiful woman of thirty who entered unannounced. This was the princess-regnant, the favourite wife of Náná Sáheb. Her features were exceedingly sweet, her complexion was clear and lustrous, and there was an expression of thought and feeling about her that greatly enhanced her loveliness; but there was something on her heart now that weighed down her beauty, the bloom of her damask cheeks had withered, her eyes were vacant and lustreless, and even her lips had lost their roses. Very anxious was that fond heart to rescue her husband from the perdition he was hunting after; but her love was not appreciated, and all her anxieties were laughed at.

The wife entered the room of her mother-in-law, and closing the door after her, sat down at her feet in silence.

'Has aught happened, my daughter, to disturb you? Why is your face so weird-like, so unusually pale?' asked the old woman of the quiet intruder.

'Mother, all over the castle I hear shouts of merriment and joy. I fear the hour of danger has arrived; I fear all my counsels have come to naught. Oh, my mother! You and I have not thought alike on this subject—we, who on all other subjects have always agreed. You have a clear mind and an unbiassed judgment. Exert them both now for your children's sake. Consider that their whole future rests on one step; pause and reflect before that step is taken, lest it be fatal.'

'Why, my daughter, what have I advised that you wish me to reconsider? Are not Náná and Bálá the rightful heirs of my husband's throne? Has not the British Government deprived them of it, most unjustly and cruelly, refusing even the petty stipend that was given to my husband? And should not they, the chosen warriors of their race, fight for their birthrights on an occasion so favourable? We, my child, are women—to us ambition is no virtue; we cannot appreciate it, because we have not the strength for action. But had you a son, would you not wish him to aspire and emulate the greatness of his ancestors?'

'To aspire? Yes; if there were the slightest chance of the aspiration being crowned with success,' said the well-judging wife. 'But, in the course that you have pointed out to your children, in the course that they are rashly, recklessly rushing upon, what chance is there of success? The British lion is as powerful as ever. Do we not know already how great is that power? How has the lesson learnt before lost its force so soon?'

'You have misread the lesson, my love,' replied the high-spirited old woman. 'We were insulted and trampled upon when our enemies were in power; all our just rights were ignored; our prayers and petitions smiled at and spurned. But fortune is on our side now. Her name is *Chanchallá*, or the ever-veering, and she has just veered round to us. If we hesitate now the cause is lost to us for ever, and mine is not the heart to waver at the hour of hope, albeit it be also the hour of danger.' Her old eyes sparkled, her lips quivered, and her whole frame was agitated as the widow of Bájee Ráo thus gently reproved the timidity of her daughter-in-law.

But the love of the young heart was steadfast; she sighed heavily and said, 'Alas! my mother, how are you sure that fickle fortune has turned round to us at last? Are you not rather blinding your better judgment, and dreaming that that has happened which you wish might happen? What is there to indicate that our conquerors are not as powerful now as before?'

'Let some one call before you the priest of Arghanáth,' replied the dowager-queen, 'and he will explain to you the revelations of the god. It is not I who in my age and weakness am inciting my children to look forward for glory and power. It is the god of our fathers, the guardian-angel of our race, that has revealed to us that our star is now in the ascendant. Hast thou not heard from thy husband that Mahádeva revealed himself to his *sabáit* in a dream, and told him that the reign of a hundred years conceded to the English is over, and that the time has arrived for driving them back to their sea?'

'Ah, mother! that was indeed a dream,' replied the wife; 'the idle dream of an idle Bráhman, who has no idea of the tempest he would evoke. But what proof have you from certain knowledge that the power of the English has declined?'

'We have certain proof even of that, my child,' said the old queen triumphantly. 'The emissaries of your husband have been to distant lands, and even to actual battlefields, and they tell us that what we fear in this country so much is a mere scarecrow, a broken reed. The English have triumphed over us here only by deceit and trickery; we have fought their battles against ourselves with our own hands; the bayonets of the sepoys only have established their throne. When those hands and those bayonets are withdrawn where will be their power?'

'This reasoning, my mother,' said her daughter-in-law, 'is at least delusive. It was the power of the English which forced our submission, and compelled the sepoys to fight their wars; that power has not ceased to exist, and think you that we are strong enough now, or ever will be, to thwart it with impunity?'

The princess had scarcely ceased when the door of the apartment was violently flung open, and the two brothers, Náná Sáheb and Bálá Sáheb, entered, and kneeled down before their mother's cushion. The wife, as is customary in Hindu families, withdrew from the presence of her male relatives to a corner of the room, while Náná, with a fierce and flashing eye, told the dowager-queen that the mutiny had broken out already at Meerut and Delhi, and asked her to bless her children, that they might declare themselves, that the Mahrattá empire might be regained. The old woman smiled a smile of heartfelt satisfaction, and kneeling down on the cushion, raised her hands to Heaven in token of thankfulness. She then arose from that posture and blessed her children in set phrase. 'Bless you, my children,' were her concluding words, 'and may Mahádeva's blessings be on you. Be bold-hearted, and remember all that you and I have suffered, that when you strike you may strike with fearful effect, for yours is a righteous cause.' The wife in the meantime had left the corner she had occupied, and flung herself at the feet of her husband in speechless fear. But it was too late; his heart was now all for ambition and war, and gently disengaging himself from her clasp, he hurried out for Cáwnpore.

CHAPTER VI. THE OUTBREAK AT CÁWNPORE

Great was the rejoicing at Cáwnpore when Náná, as a faithful subject of the Government, offered to protect the treasury and the European population generally in the event of an outbreak at that station; and every shadow of suspicion as to his intentions was removed when he actually brought down two guns and two hundred of his *Nujeebs,* or armed retainers, and placed them on guard over the treasury.

'God bless him!' exclaimed the ladies of the station. 'He is indeed a true knight, and our best of friends.'

'We only wish he may be able to do all that he promises,' said the gentlemen. 'Our only fear now is that the *budmáshes* may prove much too strong for him.'

'Ah! 'said the ladies, 'fortune favours the bold, and Náná is as brave a man as ever lived; and the Providence that has sent him to our assistance will certainly not be unmindful of us in greater need.'

Alas! that these anticipations were destined to be ruefully disappointed so soon. On the 5th of June the 2nd Light Cavalry, taking the lead in revolt, rose in a body with a shout, mounted on their horses, and left their lines, setting fire to some bungalows. The pretext urged was that they had been ill-treated by some of their officers, and yet they did not even attempt to molest their officers when, on the first alarm, they hurried to the lines. The mutineers contented themselves by breaking open the jail and setting the prisoners free, and after setting fire to some of the adjacent buildings, they marched off to Nawábgunge, intending to proceed thence to Delhi.

Náná was asleep in his quarters when Ázimoolláh Khán brought him these glad tidings.

'Up, chief! if thou wilt be a king. The hour has come at last; the 2nd Cavalry are off already.'

'Off!' exclaimed Náná, jumping out of bed and dressing hastily. 'That certainly will not suit us. We want them all here for the present. I have plenty of work for them before they go to Delhi.'

'I knew your mind, prince, and have arranged for it,' rejoined Ázimoolláh. 'The lst Native Infantry will join them in half an hour, and they will bring them back, I expect. I have not, however, been able to prevail on the miscreants of either regiment to despatch their officers. Every suggestion of that nature has been rejected by them. Nay, they have been begging their officers, and are now forcing them to get into the intrenchment. I hate sentiment in men brought up to act as butchers.'

'Oh! never mind that, Khán Báhádoor, just now,' said Náná Sáheb. 'We shall complete by and by whatever others may leave undone. But the two other regiments must rise, and that at once.'

And so it happened. Before midday the 53rd and 56th regiments also revolted. In the meantime Náná Sáheb, seizing the opportunity, took away a great portion of the money in the treasury, which he afterwards gave up to be plundered. He then went over to the rebel camp personally, to persuade the insurgents to come back and annihilate the Europeans at Cáwnpore; but they at first turned a deaf ear to all his exhortations.

'Why, my friends,' urged Náná, 'wherefore this hesitation? Was not this an original condition of our agreement? Is it not a measure absolutely necessary for our protection? Every man you leave behind will soon be placed in command of forces that will be employed in hunting you down to death. In every woman you give up heedlessly, you lose a mistress of alabaster frame.'

But these arguments made no impression, and elicited no accordant response; and Náná was well-nigh giving up the task as hopeless, when his good or evil angel, Ázimoolláh, was again at his side.

'Your wish, prince, will shortly be realized. The Golundáuzes of the 3rd Oude Horse Battery, having been disarmed, are burning to avenge the insult. They are hastening hither, and will best be able to persuade all the disaffected to the course you propose.'

The shout of the Golundáuzes was now heard from afar. 'Hur! Hur! Visheswara!' was the frantic cry, and those simple names literally electrified all the insurgents in camp, not excluding the Mahomedans, who raised the corresponding shouts of 'Deen,' and 'Alláh Akbar!'

The representations of the Golundáuzes were strongly urged, and were more successful than those of Náná Sáheb. They were not content simply to refer to the necessity of destroying the Europeans for their own protection; they also demonstrated how easily it could be effected.

'Guns, powder, and ammunition are all at hand,' said they, 'and here are the men to work them. Shall we neglect an opportunity so seasonable, and leave those guns to be used against us?'

The Golundáuzes and Náná Sáheb prevailed. Acting upon their advice, all the insurgents placed themselves under the orders of the latter, and returned to Cáwnpore; and Náná, throwing off the mask, informed General Wheeler that he had come back to attack him.

The guns were now pointed against the entrenchment within which the Europeans defended themselves. The defence was maintained heroically for twenty days, but the loss in killed and wounded within the trenches was exceedingly heavy, and the ladies and others soon became maddened by their sufferings. It was at this juncture that villainy stepped forward to the foreground and made a dupe of imbecility. We may mourn for the weakness of human nature that stooped to accept the offers of a discovered traitor, contrary to the advice and remonstrance of some of the best and bravest officers present; but we must admit that the reduced state of the besieged scarcely left them any alternative. The offer of Náná was to let all the besieged go to Alláhábád unmolested, provided they vacated the entrenchment and abandoned Cáwnpore, and made over to him all the Government money and the guns and warlike stores in the camp; and this being assented to, an agreement in writing was drawn up and signed, sealed, and ratified on both sides.

CHAPTER VII. THE DEEP DESIGN

'Well, who would have believed that Náná was such a scoundrel!' exclaimed Percival Campbell, an old inhabitant of Cáwnpore. 'Captain Moore is right; we have made the best arrangement possible under the circumstances, and may thank Heaven that we are enabled to take away our women and children to Alláhábád.'

'Don't be too sure of that yet,' said Shirn, another resident of the station, 'I don't understand Náná, and shall not be surprised if he is found in the end to be too deep for us all.'

But the suspicions of the second speaker did not appear to be well-founded. On the morning of the 27th June, a number of carts, *doolies,* and elephants were sent to the entrenchment by Náná Sáheb himself to enable the women and children and those who were sick to proceed to the river-side, and by about eight o'clock in the morning, some four hundred and fifty persons arrived there, the men and officers being permitted to take their arms and ammunition with them. Even the boats for the conveyance of the party had been provided, and were allowed to be boarded; but hardly had the fugitives taken their places in them than the boatmen, by previous arrangement, set fire to the thatched awnings of the boats and rushed to the bank, whence a heavy fire of grape and musketry was simultaneously opened. Of thirty boats which had been boarded only two had managed to start; but Náná would not allow any to escape, and one of them was swamped by round shot, while the other with the greatest difficulty was only able to proceed as far as Soorájpore, where it grounded. Those in it were after this obliged to land, and endeavoured to seek safety by flight; but two complete regiments were sent after them in pursuit. All the other boats were seized upon from both banks of the river, which was not very broad; and the men who were taken were for the most part at once put to the sword. Of the women and children several were wounded, and some of these were released from their sufferings by death, while the rest were confined in a puccá-house, called 'Subádá Kothee,' from the worst motives, a wicked old woman being appointed to persuade the helpless women to yield their persons to their villainous captor and his equally villainous followers. Both threats and hopes were freely used to induce them to comply, but to the honour of womanhood it has been recorded that there was not one female in the whole band who would accept life and liberty on such terms, all agreeing among themselves to kill each other with their teeth on the first show of violence. One young lady only had been seized upon previously by a trooper of the 2nd Light Cavalry, and carried off to his own quarters, where she was violently treated; but, finding a favourable opportunity, she rose up at night, and securing her ravisher's sword, avenged herself by killing him and three others, after which she flung herself into a well, and was killed. Another little child, a girl of six years, having been separated from her mother, and having received a sword-cut on the thigh, was taken up by a trooper, who expressed a wish to adopt her, he being childless. But Náná was aghast at the idea of a European child—even one—being thus saved, and the trooper was imprisoned for his temerity, the child being committed to the *Subádá Kothee* for such destiny as was reserved for the rest.

Great was the pleasure of Náná Sáheb at the success of his treacherous and cowardly enterprise. At the sunset of the same day a general review of all his troops was made, and salutes were fired, the first, being of twenty-one guns, in honour of himself as Peishwá of Southern India; the second, of nineteen guns, in honour of Bálá Sáheb as Governor-General under him; and the third, of seventeen guns, for Jowállá Prasád, a resaldár, who was appointed Brigadier and Commander-in-chief of Náná's forces. It was also simultaneously proclaimed by beat of drums throughout Cáwnpore and its districts that Náná had entirely conquered the English, whose period of sovereignty in India had expired. The celebrated proclamations were next issued one after another, the first of which referred to the wish of Queen Victoria that all her subjects should be made Christians, the attempt made in accordance with that wish to convert the native army by serving out cartridges smeared with the fat of pigs and bullocks, the failure of the plan, and the total extermination of the British reinforcements, while on their way out from England, by the combined attack made on them in Egypt by the Sultán of Turkey and the Khedive. The second proclamation, assuming the royal tone, assured the people of protection, comfort, and ease, and exhorted them to carry on their respective avocations in perfect confidence as heretofore; and a third called upon all subjects and landholders to be obedient to the new Ráj, and on all the officers of the Government to collect the balances of revenue on its behalf, threatening recusants with punishment. In the meantime Náná continued to receive large additions to his forces from all sides, mutineers from every direction, who had heard of his great achievements, pouring into Cáwnpore with great alacrity; and to feed and otherwise provide for these, depredations of every kind were freely resorted to, notwithstanding the vaunting notifications which had been issued—the *mahájuns,* or merchants, being reduced to beggary, and the poorer classes almost driven out of their homes.

CHAPTER VIII. THE REFUGE

We now turn to the fugitives who had gained the village of Soorájpore. They were in all fourteen in number, and were hotly pursued till they found breathing-time and a temporary refuge in the small temple of Káli, which we have previously described. Their pursuers then brought a gun to bear on the temple, but finding that this made no impression on it, they began to heap up firewood before the doorway, and then set fire to the pile, adding a small quantity of powder to it, the smoke from which compelled the fugitives to sally and take towards the river again. The crowd around them was very great; six of the fugitives were soon cut down, and two others were shot through. Of the rest two ran into the crowd and were not traced; while the other four threw themselves into the river and swam down some six miles, till they were hailed by the retainers of a friendly rájáh, Digbejay Sing of Baiswárrá, by whom they were protected and fed, and eventually escorted to the camp of Brigadier-General Havelock when he went to Cáwnpore.

'Well, Mackenzie, what are we to do now?' asked one of the two fugitives who had been separated from the rest, of his companion in peril. The speaker was a man of about forty years, having a very sinister and undignified appearance, which was however counterbalanced by an extra share of cunning and hypocrisy, which formed the chief traits of his character, and were marked unmistakably on his face.

'Why, Bernard, I suppose we must run for our lives,' answered his companion, a younger man, and of a larger and stronger frame, whose well-developed audacity and insolence had subsided for the moment to the dangers of his position. 'Or perhaps it would be better if we could find shelter here for a time with the villagers.'

'But who will give us shelter here? Don't you see that all the men around us are arrayed on the side of Náná?'

'Yes, the men are, but not the women. We can have little indeed to hope for from the men; but the kinder sympathies of the female heart may yet befriend us. Look sharp, Bernard, and tell me if you see any women by themselves.'

As if Providence intended especially to befriend them in their flight the first turn of the road, which separated them from their pursuers, brought them before the range of clean huts we described when referring to the

Dasahárá ceremonies; and the same persons who were then at the door were there at this moment also, occupied almost in the same avocations as before. The boy, however, the hope of the family, had no sooner caught sight of the Europeans than he ran into the house to hide himself; and the two women also rose up in haste to follow him. This has been and still is the position of Englishmen in India. They do not feel in common with the races they have conquered; there is no sympathy on one side, and no confidence on the other. The women scamper off in fear whenever they see English faces in their vicinity; the children look up towards them with alarm; and even the men never come to ask for any favour or assistance from them in their difficulties, if they can help it. There is no bond of union between the two races: there has been no attempt to establish any; and yet much wonder is expressed that the natives are not faithfully attached to their conquerors. Here were two fugitive Europeans in the midst of a hostile village, and yet the first impulse of both the women and children upon whom they came unawares was to run off from their presence.

'Mother, we are sore beset. Save us; have pity on our sufferings,' prayed the man called Bernard of the old lady of the huts; but she ran off to the inner apartments without vouchsafing any reply to his appeal, which probably she did not understand.

'You, angel of goodness!' exclaimed Mackenzie, addressing the younger lady, 'you also are a mother. For your son's and your husband's sake, and for the sake of our common Father in Heaven, save and shelter us.'

The woman did not understand a word of what was told to her; but she well understood the position of the fugitives, and the manner of the appeal made a deep impression on her mind. Without attempting to say anything in reply to it, she merely pointed to the door which she wished them to enter, and following them, she barricaded it within, and then conducted the fugitives to the cow-house, where they were left concealed behind huge heaps of straw.

Such is woman's generous heart! The same female, it will be remembered, had before refused a night's rest to the emissary of Náná, on the plea that her husband was not at home; but there was not a moment's hesitation on her part to screen two fugitives, albeit of a foreign and feared race, who were running for their lives.

The mother remonstrated with her daughter for admitting them. It was unsafe, she said, to shelter the enemies of Náná Sáheb; and for two lone women to live within the same compound with two strong and desperate men of an alien race was exceedingly indiscreet. The simple reply of the daughter was: 'Mother, these men are in momentary danger of their lives. If we don't screen them they are sure to be murdered. The risk to us is very great; but God, who sees everything, will protect us while we protect them.' It has often been said that the natives throughout the country were hostile towards their rulers during these disturbances. It has been conveniently forgotten that every man or woman that was saved was protected by the natives who were friendly to them.

'What a jewel of a woman this black beauty is!' exclaimed Mackenzie from his quiet retreat between two large bundles of straw. 'She is worth her weight in gold!'

'Or of a place in the ancient hall of the Mackenzies, as the wife of a truant son of St. Andrew? Is that what you are thinking of?'

'No,' said Mackenzie, with a sneer. 'A nigger is a nigger to me for all her virtues. But to tell the truth, Bernard, I would not mind snatching a kiss from those ripe lips, though I may not wish to have her for my wife.'

'That's my idea too,' responded his companion. 'The girl is a brave one though, and it is a pity that she is lost on a nigger husband, who cannot possibly appreciate her worth.'

'Well, she has done us a good service; suppose we do one to her in return, and carry her off from her ourang-outang? That would not be a loss to her to mope at, surely?'

'But what shall we do with her? We cannot well have her in common between us, you know.'

'Why not?' said Mackenzie. 'There is no harm in that when the woman is a nigger, you know. It would be a different thing if she were a European.'

'True enough,' responded Bernard. 'Well, we shall put our two heads together, and see how we can manage it.'

CHAPTER IX. TRIUMPH, DOUBTS, AND FEARS

The guns went merrily off from the ramparts of the castle of Bithoor, when Náná, in the height of his glory, visited it on the 2nd of July. A salute of a hundred guns was fired in honour of the Emperor of Delhi, now announced as the Emperor of all India; one of eighty guns was fired to the memory of Bájee Ráo, the putative father of Náná Sáheb and late ex-Peishwá of Poona; one of sixty guns in honour of Náná himself, as Peishwá of Southern India; one of twenty-one guns in honour of the Queen-dowager of Pooná, the widow of Bájee Ráo; and another of the same number in honour of the Queen-regnant, Náná's favourite wife.

'The bright stars never lie!' said the Queen-dowager, as she heard the thundering of the guns, and turned a smiling face towards her daughter-in-law, whose countenance was still pensive and overcast. 'Has not the prophecy of Dássá Bábá, our revered Gooroo, been fulfilled at last?'

'No, mother, do not deceive yourself. The danger is only becoming more imminent.'

'Why, my child, the Hanumán-horoscope of eight angles, which the sage prepared for your husband, was verified by Náná personally. After seven days of prayer he slept on it, as he was directed to do, whereupon Hanumán revealed himself to him in a dream and assured him of complete success in all his undertakings. And has not this come to pass already? Has not Cáwnpore been wrenched from the English for ever?'

'Not for ever, mother! The clouds move on and come back again. If the English have abandoned Cáwnpore, they are sure to reoccupy it.'

'But who will reoccupy it, my daughter? Our enemies have been killed and rooted out, and both Dássá Bábá and Dabeedeen pronounce the triumph to be ominous.'

'Ominous? Yes, "Ominous", mother, is the word. Ominous of much evil in the future, I fear. Don't forget, mother, the fable of our country, that every drop of a Rákshasa's blood gives birth to a separate Rákshasa to replace the dead fiend. The English are descended from the Rákshases, and every drop of English blood that has been shed is sure to raise us a new enemy.'

'You dream, my child, and discompose yourself unnecessarily with your dreams. If the English are powerful, so are we.'

'I dream indeed, mother, as you say; or rather, I have dreamt as the priest of Árganáth and my husband have dreamt. But mine has been a fearful dream, and I must reveal it. I sought for my husband and our kinsmen in my sleep: I found them not in the castle of Bithoor, which I saw had been burnt to the ground; I sought for them in the ancient palaces of Pooná, but they were not there. In the untold depths of an unknown forest, in which man had never set foot before, with the hungry tiger hunting for him on one side, and the vengeful Briton closing upon him from another, I saw my beloved husband abandoned and alone. I have knelt daily and nightly to Mahádeva to avert this awful fate from him; but no cheering smile have I been able to read on Iswara's face even in my dream.'

'Your dream is naught, my child, and had birth only in your fears. Give not to the light a cloud so dark that suits darkness only. The god of our country cannot so desert his own soldier in the hour of his need. He fights on our side already, and at this moment has crowned us with triumph. Damp not your husband's ardour with your fears.'

At this moment the queen of the Peishwá was called away by a female servant sent to her by her husband. Wan, haggard, and almost spectral was the face of the loving wife as she flung her arms around the neck of her truant lord; nor was Nánà unmindful of her condition.

'Ah! my beloved, what has disturbed your mind so much as to reduce you to this state? Speak, dearest, what grief sits heavy on your heart? Nánà would be dead indeed before he ceases to feel for you.'

A shade passed over her delicate features, and she sighed heavily.

'You have put your foot in the lion's den, my lord,' said she; 'how will you get it out unscathed?'

'The lion's den! Is that your fear? Why, love, the lion you dread is an old and feckless one, whose teeth have all been drawn out. Our hearts are bold, our arms are strong, and Mahádeva has blessed our cause already. Don't you fret yourself in fear.'

'The cause is a blessed one, I know; but oh! my husband, the arms of the white man are much stronger than yours. The English lion is not so toothless as you fancy, and you have outrun the bounds of discretion in lashing him up to rage. Beware, my lord, of the fatal spring!'

'The spring! He will never spring, my love; we have cut all his tendons, and he cannot stand.'

'Not so, my lord; you have only cut the chain that tethered him down to peace; untied him for the spring that must surely follow. Your only safety now is in flight. Save me, my lord, by saving yourself; save us all before it is too late. If we fly now to Poonà under feigned names, and keep ourselves apart from the commotions at hand, we may yet be pardoned and spared.'

'Pardoned and spared! Are these words befitting the Peishwá's queen in the hour of her husband's triumph? Speak them not, love, for they do not become either you or me. 'Tis I that have raised all the tempest around us; almost I alone. For this purpose I visited Calpie, Delhi, and Lucknow. The Emperor of Delhi and the Begum of Oude are but puppets in my hand. And shall I leave them to enjoy that success which my wit and my prowess have so nearly secured?'

'You dream, my lord, when you speak of success. You have killed the English soldiers in Cáwnpore. Is the English nation less strong for it than they were? Where are your arms and your soldiers, my lord? Will the old man of Delhi fight? He cannot if he would. Is the Begum strong enough to support you? Were she ten times more willing than she is, she has not the power to do so. Can the mutinous sepoys be depended upon? They have deceived one master, and will not be more faithful to another. Believe me, I do not speak simply from fear. I am a Mahrattá, my lord, as well as you are; the women of our country have always fought alongside of their husbands and their brethren. I, too, grieve for the debasement of our country as you do, for our past glory, our lost name.[22] But I see further than you do in this matter, my lord. I see plainly that the storm you have raised will only level you with the dust, and with you all the fortresses, towers, and opposition you have called forth. Oh, my lord, you have recklessly taken your stand on the brink of a precipice. Stop, or you are undone for ever!'

'Hush! dearest lady, hush! Nor raise again those doubts which I have struggled so hard to pacify. I will not say that your fears are groundless. But thus must not think the wife of Náná Sáheb, far less Náná himself. I have rushed too far forward now to go back. A throne or death, no matter how it comes, is the hazard of the die. I know the precipice on which I stand; but I may not recede now from my doom. Nor, lady, could Pooná, or any other place in India, give us that shelter which you wish me to seek.'

'And why was this fearful position sought for and assumed?' asked the wife.

'It is my destiny that has led me on,' was Náná's reply.

'Then are we undone indeed!' said the wife, and sobbed heavily on his breast.

CHAPTER X. THE MASSACRE

The arrival of a British force at Futtehpore obliged Náná Sáheb to take the offensive sooner than he would have wished it. He sent ten thousand troops against this force, but they were soon beaten back. Reinforcement after reinforcement was despatched to aid them; but to no effect. At last Náná himself headed a fresh party, and proceeded to the seat of war, which had already approached within twenty miles of Cáwnpore; but he found so little chance of success that he was obliged to run back to the station with all his followers. This retrograde movement spread such panic all around that, leaving house and property, every man who had a hand in the rebellion took to his heels, many deserting even their families in their eagerness to escape with their lives. The sepoys in particular, laden with immense booty, were the first to disperse in every direction. Nor could Náná afford to stay behind them, though he would not leave till he had completed the dastardly atrocity he had planned from the outset.

Just after their defeat at Futtehpore the rebels had captured a few poor natives, who were brought in to Náná as having been the bearers of letters supposed to have been written to the British commander by the helpless females kept imprisoned in the *Subádá Kothee*.

'Ha !' exclaimed Náná, 'and so there has been surreptitious correspondence between our prisoners and our enemies? Put all the go-betweens to the sword to begin with—we shall deal with the prisoners presently.'

'A little respite is necessary, king,' said Bábá Bhut, one of Náná's general-superintendents. 'I have information that some of the *Mahájuns* and

Bengalee Báboos in the city are implicated with the spies, and I would trace out these before destroying the evidence against them.'

'Seize all the Báboos and *Mahájuns*,' said Nániá; 'we want no evidence against them. They must all be more or less implicated; nor does it matter if they are not. Let the spies be cut down at once, as I have ordered. Of the Báboos who write English we had better cut off their right-hands and noses; and the same punishment will also do for the *Mahájuns*, unless they can purchase their liberty at a fair price. Some English prisoners have also been taken from Futtehgurh; these may be shot.'

The orders of the pseudo-Peishwá were carried out at once. The so-called spies, or go-betweens, were put to the sword, and the English prisoners shot to death. After this the women confined in the *Subádá Kothee* were ordered to come out, but neither threats nor persuasion could induce them to do so.

'We can die here together,' said one of them. 'Our enemy is relentless, there is no hope for us here or beyond these walls. But here, dying together, we shall at least be safe from indignity.'

'But there is no fear of any indignity, Mem,' said Nániá's emissary. 'No one will harm you if you will come out quietly; otherwise you will all be dragged out with a rude hand, and no sort of insult will be spared.'

While he spoke he seized one of the women to exemplify the threat he had launched out; but all the other prisoners came to her aid, and so laid hold of each other, and clung so close that it was impossible to separate them or to drag them out together. This being reported to Nániá he ordered some troopers to shoot at them from the doors and windows; while others rushed upon them with swords and bayonets. Then was commenced that butchery which has never perhaps been equalled. Many of the poor, helpless creatures fell down in their agony at the feet of their murderers, and asked to be spared. But, even if the ruffians had wished to spare them, they had no power to do so. The massacre was deliberately completed in the midst of the most dreadful shrieks and cries, which were heard from a great distance. There were about one hundred and forty or one hundred and fifty souls in the *Kothee*, including the children, and from a little before sunset till after nightfall, the whole time was occupied in killing them. Groans! Has any murderer ever been disturbed by groans? These murderers at least were not. The piercing cry of children! Has it ever arrested the uplifted arm of an assassin? These assassins at least did not acknowledge the spell. They went through their fearful work untroubled either by cries or groans, stopping only at candle-light, when the building was locked up for the night, and the murderers went to their homes.

After that night of horror came a morning as bright and cheerful as any that had preceded it. How long was it allowed to remain so? The doors of the

Kothee being opened, it was found that some ten or fifteen females and a few children had found shelter under the murdered bodies of their fellow-prisoners, and so escaped death. Were these to be spared? The fiend in a human form shrieked 'No!' and fresh orders were given to terminate their lives. But they were not able to bear the idea of being cut down as their associates had been; the horrors of the previous night were maddening, and they all rushed out as one man into the compound, and seeing a well there, threw themselves into it without hesitation. Poor brave English hearts! brave even to the last! Brave women and brave children! In what page of history shall we read an account to equal your heroic sufferings? Nor was the ferocity of the fiend yet glutted. The dead bodies of those who had been murdered inside the house were now dragged out like those of dogs, and thrown over the living into the well; after which the cowards moved on, and the station was deserted. On the following morning Cáwnpore was reoccupied by the English forces under Havelock, and then arose the cry from all ranks, and the vain regret that they had come, alas, too late!

CHAPTER XI. THE REQUITAL

Bernard and Mackenzie were well fed by their hostess before they retired for the night to their straw-pallets in the cow-house at Soorájpore. When the night had advanced further a sudden cry of alarm was heard in the village, that a large party of soldiers had entered it in search of fugitives. Both the old woman and her daughter, startled from their sleep, rose up in fear, the latter clasping her boy in her arms.

'Oh, Mahádeva!' exclaimed she in fear; 'is it a crime to shelter and to save? Oh, mother, what shall we do now? Surely the soldiers will be searching every house for the fugitives, and what will become of us when they are found?'

'Hush!' said the old woman. 'The mistake we have made cannot now be repaired. We should not have sheltered the fugitives. But since we have done so we must allay suspicion by boldness and lies. This is not your work. Go, hide yourself where you best may, and leave me alone to go through this trial, or rather, leave the boy with me, as I must meet the soldiers with him.'

With that the old woman, holding an earthen lamp in one hand and the boy by the other, proceeded towards the door of the house just when the soldiers had halted before it with a roar.

'Open the door,' said the foremost of the party, 'or we shall batter it down and set fire to your homestead;' and with the threat came a furious knock on the door that almost unhinged it.

With steady hands the old woman unbarred the latch.

'What is your will, sirs?' said she, with well-affected surprise and fear.

'What may your will be with an old woman and her grandchild?'

'Who else have you got in the house now?' was the question asked in reply.

'None other, sirs, at present. The father of this boy and his uncle have gone to the marts in Alláhábád to sell grain. I am expecting them every day, but they have not come back yet, and so we are living only by ourselves.'

'I believe you, old lady,' said one of the throng, evidently a man in authority; 'for I was in this place before, and begged for a night's shelter from you, which you did not grant. She is not likely, friends, to house strangers of a foreign race when she curtly refused to house me. Nay, mother, I bear you no grudge for that; but you have told us one fib to-night, for surely the mother of that boy is in the house.'

'Never mind the mother of the boy now,' said the leader of the party, who was no other than Bálá Sáheb himself; 'we have plenty of work before us; move on!' and with another boisterous shout the party moved on, while the old woman with now trembling hands fastened her door in haste.

Bernard and Mackenzie had both come out of their hiding-place, and had armed themselves to sell their lives dearly; but they were thankful that the occasion for defence had been so adroitly postponed.

'Thou hast the calm aspect of a heroine, mother,' said Bernard; 'and I wish I had my purse by me to repay such service adequately.'

'We want no payment, soldiers. Money does not repay good acts. Go to your beds again, and may the rest of your sleep be undisturbed. Early in the morning you must leave our place.'

But here her daughter interposed. 'We send them to certain destruction, mother, if we send them away immediately after their pursuers. Give them another day, that, when the roads are clear of loiterers, they may escape in safety.'

'Be it so, my child, if you wish it; but while they remain here our danger is not over.'

And so they remained, the incarnate fiends, in that home of innocence, to plot mischief against those poor creatures who were incurring so much peril for their sakes. A second night on their pallets of straw enabled them to ripen their scheme of baseness and ingratitude, and to develope [sic] it. The night was dark. The traitors broke open the room in which the females slept. A woman's shriek—an unavailing struggle! Oh merciful Heaven! why is crime triumphant in the world?

The old woman shrieked for aid. 'Help! murder! Save us, neighbours,' was the cry; but the neighbours were all fast asleep, and very few heard that cry of fear. The boy ran out in terror to hide himself; he understood not the nature of the outrage that was consummated. The victim struggled hard, but in vain; when the violence was completed she was insensible as a corpse.

And then the ruffians fled, the old woman running after them, though she was twice pelted at, calling upon all the villagers to rise up against them. But there were none to arrest their steps, and when the villagers did get up the criminals had already made good their retreat.

And how did the village community think and speak of the matter? Some expressed horror at the crime; others vowed vengeance, but in bated breath; while others condemned in unmeasured terms the indiscretion of the women that had resulted in such outrage. But the old woman did not stop to listen to their comments. With a heavy heart she recrossed her threshold, and locking the door doubly, proceeded to the bedside of the sufferer. She was surprised to find her greatly recovered, but she also saw on her face an unnatural calm, which contrasted fearfully with her ordinary sweetness.

'Cheer up, my child,' said she. 'With the morning I myself shall go in quest of Bálá Sáheb, and direct him against the fugitives. Believe me, your wrongs shall be avenged.'

'No, mother; we are too poor to think of vengeance: our lot is to suffer. I was indiscreet in sheltering them, and my indiscretion has been severely punished. Mother, let me die. Take this boy, mother, from me, and make him over to his father. Tell him that I was true to him to the last, and that he must be true to our hapless child. Give my love to my brother. Mother, so long as you live be kind to my son. Men cannot love children as women can.'

'But why do you speak, my daughter, in that desponding tone? Yours was not the crime. Your husband is devotedly attached to you, and will not cast you away for the violence you have suffered. Why do you speak of leaving us, my child? I do not understand your words. What are you thinking of?'

The wife shuddered when her husband's love for her was alluded to. 'Mother, I am no longer worthy of him. Seek him out and my brother early in the morning, that my funeral ceremonies may be performed by those who were dearest to me. I have swallowed all the rat's-bane that was in the house, and feel the effects of the poison in my veins already.'

The strength which had buoyed her up was now exhausted; her head drooped, her eyes dilated, and the next moment she was a corse. And then there was a howl from the old woman that brought again all the villagers to her door; and the door was forced open, and there was the hurrying to and fro of many footsteps, and the peering of many eyes over the corse—over the poor violated woman that lay unavenged!

Chapter XII. The Flight from Bithoor

It was on the morning of the 17th of July that, Cáwnpore having been recaptured by General Havelock, Nán̄á Sáheb returned once more to Bithoor. He had still a large force with him, and many guns; but his men were thoroughly disheartened and disorganized, and they were deserting him in numbers.

'Mother, our luck is over,' said Nán̄á Sáheb, addressing the widow of Bájee Ráo. 'The soldiers murmur loudly, though they have taken more booty than we have got. For us there is no safety, I fear, except in flight.'

'Flight! while the stars give you a throne? That must not be, my son. Be of bold heart; fresh troops will join us ere noon, and Cáwnpore will be regained. If not, with our castle fully manned we shall yet be able to defy the English general and his forces here at Bithoor.'

'No, mother, no; our followers are utterly prostrated, and we are too weak for defence. Our best course now is to proceed to Lucknow.'

'And there seek protection under the coif of a dissipated Begum? Is it thus speaks Nán̄á Sáheb, the adopted son of Bájee Ráo? Then is the Mahrattá cause lost indeed for ever!'

Nán̄á remained silent under the rebuke for a time, then slowly asked, 'Will it please you, mother, if I remain here to be betrayed? Every man in our following has a secret project of his own. Save you, mother, and my wife, I have no one on whom I can rely.'

'That is always the fate of kings, my son. Make it their interest to stand by you, and you will force all your followers to be faithful to you. Give them everything that you can afford; promise them more in the future. The cunning workman makes use of the most dangerous tools with safety.'

'Every shift and expedient, mother, have I tried—every promise have I exhausted; but they waver still. They are grumbling on all sides, and are deserting rapidly. Deceive not yourself, mother; we remain in Bithoor but to die.'

'And if it be so, my son, even then would I wish you to remain here to fight and die. If you are the last man at the guns, take your stand there and fight on, and I at least will not desert or betray you. You have no mercy to expect from the white man; you can die without asking for any.'

'I could do that, mother; but our cause is not so desperate yet. Havelock fights hard; the devil of the Christians guides his blade. But the cause of the English is not so hopeful in other places, and our reverse here may yet be remedied if we can only throw more strength into Lucknow.'

'Be it so then, my son. But remember that Nán̄á at Lucknow becomes only the coadjutor of a Mahomedan king, not a king himself.'

'Not so, my mother. The partitions of the empire have been secured to us severally by treaty. Kings assist each other without detriment to their rights.'

'Were the whole empire in your grasp, my son, you would think otherwise; and so will Huzrut Mul and Mummoo Khán, when they find themselves able to throw you off. But that matters not at present. If we must leave Bithoor, I care little whether we go to Delhi or Lucknow.'

During this conference between mother and son the greatest consternation was spreading all over Bithoor, sure tidings having been received that the English at Cáwnpore were making mighty preparations to attack it.

'Not an hour is to be lost,' said Ázimooláh. 'Send word to the Peishwá in the zenáná. Let him come out at once and arrange for our fight.'

Náná received this message in his wife's apartment, where the two were communing together. He had the greatest difficulty in breaking to her the tidings of their danger, and did it as tenderly as his nature would permit.

'It was this, this that I foresaw, my dear lord,' exclaimed she, when she understood their exact position; 'this indeed that I was afraid of. It has come on sooner even than I expected. But are you prepared for the occasion, my lord?'

'I am. Your lips chide me not, my love, your heart feels for me, and I am certain I can be happy with you in any position. Nor is all hope lost to us yet. Though we are obliged to abandon Bithoor now, all our prospects are not closed at once; and I still expect to make you the queen of the Mahrattá throne ere long, and never brow better deserved a royal diadem than thine.'

'Abandon that thought, my lord, and everything may yet go on well. Think not of thrones or states. Our good mother is ambitious; I am not. Devise only how we may be safe and happy in a quiet, private life. We have already compromised ourselves fearfully; no place within British territory will perhaps screen us altogether from danger. But there are lands beyond India, where we may lead a safe and humble life; and I in any place and position will be happy with you, my lord. Cut yourself off from the meshes that entangle you, and then indeed would I not regret the difficulties that surround us.'

Náná was almost unmanned by the unreproaching love of his wife, and he held down his head, unable to reply. At this moment Bálá Sáheb burst into the room.

'Come, brother, come. Our moments are very precious now. In a short time even our retreat may be cut off.'

Very hurried were the preparations which were made for their flight. The troops were allowed to disperse on all sides, and repair by different routes to Lucknow; and the pseudo-Peishwá left the castle of Bithoor with a small retinue only. He had barely time to escape. Bithoor was occupied by the English immediately after, and the palace burnt to the ground.

CHAPTER XIII. THE BEREAVED

The fugitives from Soorájpore had fled on through darkness with the speed of the hunted deer, and were proceeding in the direction of Futtehpore, where they expected to fall in with the English army. By the time that they were half-way to it the dawn was breaking slowly over the meadows, and they shortly after saw a cart jolting over the ruts of a lonely road.

'It would be a relief to us if we could make the cartmen turn round and take us to Futtehpore,' said Bernard.

'But they won't, I think,' replied Mackenzie: 'and we must not attempt to force them, as that would attract attention.'

'You are right, perhaps, Mackenzie; but my feet are bleeding, and I cannot stir my stumps. Are we to lie down here and die?'

Mackenzie was silent, as if in thought. In the meantime the cart drew nearer, and they found that it was empty, there being only two men on it, apparently peasants, who had disposed of their goods and were returning home. Both of them were stalwart, sinewy men, though possibly not more courageous than Hindu bumpkins generally are.

'Ahem, carters,' hailed Mackenzie; 'will you take us to Futtehpore for hire?'

'No,' replied the peasants. 'We are just returning thence, and are anxious to go home.'

'But we must have your cart at any rate. Your feet are in excellent condition, and you can easily walk home, while ours are in miserable plight. Will you lend or sell us your cart?'

'We cannot afford to do either, though we are averse to say "nay" to Englishmen in distress.'

'Ah, my friends. In this country it is the rule with us Englishmen to impress the carts we require for service, and you know well that very few would care to pay you a *cowrie* for the carriage they would take away from you by force. But we here are more considerate, and you should not be unreasonable with us.'

'Well, sirs, as for impressing our cart, you could not do so just at present without raising the whole country against you; and you know that that would not be a safe game for you. But we do not wish to be unreasonable, and will give up our cart and bullocks if you will pay a fair price for them.'

This was agreed to with alacrity, and the men, who had elsewhere affected not to have their purses with them, were now glad enough to fork out the money that was asked for. The cart with its new occupants then turned back in the direction of Futtehpore, while the peasants pursued their onward journey on foot.

'I am afraid, Probhoo, that we have not done right in giving up our cart to those men. Mischief is written on their faces. Either they are flying from it, or are hastening to it.'

'That does not concern us, Shunkur. We find them in difficult straits, and help them without loss to ourselves. There is nothing wrong so far as that goes. If they are after mischief, or have been in it, a cart and a pair of bullocks will not help them out of it long.'

Thus spake the husband and brother of the poor suicide of Soorájpore, not knowing what fearful mischief those miscreants had made in their own household; and when they did know of it where were the wretches again to be found? They had mixed with the rest of the English forces at Futtehpore, and had marched on thence to other places.

For three days, three long, unending days, did Shunkur remain bereft of strength and reason. These were followed by a longer interval of fierce and burning fever, disturbed by incoherent ravings. But he was well tended, his brother-in-law Probhoo scarcely ever stirring from his side, while his mother-in-law attended to all those wants to which women know how best to minister. At last his sickness left him, and health and intellect were regained—regained for one purpose only, the thought of which electrified his debilitated frame—Revenge!

'I have sworn, Probhoo, that I will avenge her untimely and fearful end. Tarry you here at home and protect your mother and my son. My destiny leads me on to an appointed doom.'

'Not so, Shunkur; you shall not go alone. I too have sworn revenge. Our mother must look after the child as she may, and neighbours will help them both. Our enemies are strong; we must go together against them.'

And so it was arranged. But the great difficulty was to find out where the miscreants were. During Shunkur's long illness the English forces had been marching hither and thither in all directions from Alláhábád. How were the ruffians to be found? The relief of the garrison at Lucknow was at this time the principal aim of the English in this quarter. Would the ravishers be among the reinforcements sent thither?

'We can only hunt for them in the dark, my brother,' said Probhoo; 'we don't even know their names, and to trace out two Englishmen by their faces, out of so many scattered all over the country, will be a very difficult affair.'

'We must do it nevertheless, my brother. We have sworn to devote our lives to the search.'

'Hist! I hear a step. I hope it is of some one who can help us in this strait.'

The intruder was an elderly but well-made man, having a calm and even noble aspect, though it was somewhat worn and thoughtful.

'Can I have a night's shelter anywhere here, my friends?' asked he.

'Yes, if you will tell us who you are and whither you are bound,' was the reply of Probhoo.

'It is hardly fair to insist on a condition like that,' said the stranger. 'We are unknown to each other, and can have no concern in each other's affairs, and the times are troublesome, when brother scarcely trusts his brother with his affairs.'

'The greater the need that we should know whom we shelter. Our household has suffered already by sheltering strangers.'

'May I ask of what race they were?'

'Accursed Englishmen!' was the bitter response of Shunkur. 'Cowardly ruffians, who have brought shame and misery where there was nothing but happiness and peace.'

'And have the traitors escaped?'

'Yes; for we were not at home. But if there be a God in heaven our day must come!'

'Let us pray that it may,' said the stranger; 'and accept me as one of yourselves, oh my friends, for our cause is the same. I will tell you my story, and hear yours in return; and, if you will give me a night's rest with you, it may be that we may decide upon hunting our game together.'

The shelter asked for was given, and a friend of great value was found in the stranger.

CHAPTER XIV. THE HÁVILDÁR'S STORY

The story of the new-comer was as follows: — 'He was a Hávildár, attached to the 10th Regiment N. I., stationed at Futtehgurh. That regiment had never intended to mutiny, and the men were steadfastly attached to their colours. On the Queen's Birthday, the 24th of May, they received a letter from a friend at Áchánuk (Barrackpore), a place ten miles distant from Calcutta, stating that there had been a quarrel at that station between a Chámár (workman in leather) and a sepoy, the former of whom had asked for water to drink, which the latter had indignantly refused. 'How can I give you water,' said the sepoy, 'when you belong to the Chámár caste; and how dare you ask it of me knowing that I am a Kshetriya?' 'When the Kshetriyas,' replied the Chámár, 'do not hesitate to bite off with their teeth the cartridges which I lubricate with the fat of cows and pigs, it is mere affectation on their part to refuse a drop of water to a poor man on the plea of caste.' This was followed by more angry words on both sides, after which a conciliatory inquiry was made, which resulted in the discovery, by several sepoys together, of Chámárs being actually employed, at a short distance from the cantonment where the cartridges were made, in smearing them with the obnoxious grease. This news was received with different feelings by different men in the regiment. Some believed in its truth, others received it with distrust; but they all remained silent over it for the time.

'A short while after the regiment received a second letter, which came from Bareilly, in which it was stated that it had been ascertained at Delhi that with the *áttá* (flour) supplied for the use of the sepoys were mixed the ground bones of cows and pigs; that the shopkeepers had been prohibited from selling *áttá* of any other kind; and that bones were also mixed with salt and sugar. A third letter, received from the same quarter, stated that with the *ghee* (melted butter) given to the men was mixed the fat of cows and pigs.

'There were still some men in the regiment, and among them myself,' said the Hávildár, 'who did not believe in these stories. But we people of India are steadfastly attached to our religion; and the Company Báhádoor, our former masters, had respected us for this. We therefore went in a body to our officers to show them the letters that had come to us, and to ask them to enlighten us with their knowledge on the subjects referred to, as we were still loath to believe that the information as it had come to us was wholly true. Well, what was the answer they gave us? They called us a parcel of donkeys; said that our feelings towards the Government were already suspected; and threatened on the display of any sort of recusancy to disarm us.

'At this juncture came in amongst us the well-known *chuppáties*, a kind of fiery-cross sent by Náná Sáheb to stir us up to action. These cakes were said to have originated with Dássá Bábá, the spiritual guide of the Bithoor family, who, having read Náná's fortune in the stars, made a *jádoo*, or charm, which he reduced into pills, and having made an immense number of cakes, put a pill into each, the cakes being carried all over the country to extend the force of the charm among those by whom they were received. We, however, refused to encourage these attempts, and the *chuppáties* sent to us were returned.

'The next message transmitted to us came in the name of Náná himself. He advised us that we were suspected, that British troops were marching on us, and that on their arrival at the station we would be disarmed. This was the threat that our officers had virtually hinted at when we proffered our first complaint; it therefore made a deep impression on the credulity of the men throughout the regiment, and, a council having been convened by them to consider the measures that should be taken, a fresh representation to our officers was determined upon.

'I was one of the spokesmen chosen. I took off my cap before the major, and exhibited to him this sword-cut on my head; I bared my right arm before him, and showed him how it had been nearly severed by another wound; I pointed to this bullet-hole through my left elbow. All these wounds, I said, I had received in fighting the battles of my masters; and I asked if it was true that we were now suspected, and were to be disarmed? The reply was that I was an old fool, and that if we did correspond with Náná Sáheb we deserved to be disarmed and punished. I ventured to remonstrate. We had not, I said, corresponded with Náná Sáheb; it was he who had been sending us *chuppáties* and letters; but he had received no answer from us to any of his communications. I laid stress also on the general fidelity of the regiment; on the many fights we had fought, on the many honours we had won. "What better guarantee of good conduct," said I, "can you expect from us than this, that while we are serving in one regiment, our children are serving in others? There are three of my sons, major, now in Her Majesty's service." "And can you tell us how many of them have turned traitors already? Will you show us the letters you have received from them lately?" My blood boiled within me to resent this cowardly insult; but I controlled my feelings, and simply answered that all my sons were stanch and true, and that not one of the regiments to which they belonged had rebelled. But the reply was received with an insolent smile of incredulity; and I well believe that it is treatment like this that has made traitors of us all.

'On the 16th of June the Subadár of the 41st Regiment, which had recently come from Seetápore, and was located a few miles distant from us across the river, reported that the men of the regiment had risen and murdered their officers, and asked us to do the same. Still true to our salt, we placed this letter before our colonel, and said that we had written back in reply that we would abide by our faithfulness, and that they had better not come in our way, as we would certainly oppose them. But we were still regarded with distrust. A little show of confidence even now would have strengthened the fidelity of the regiment; but this was withheld, and on my remonstrating with a junior officer on this point I was—will you believe it, brethren?—struck by him with a cane. That blow has made me a rebel; that insult can only be wiped out with the coward's blood. After this the whole regiment rebelled, the greater portion of it crossing over at once to Oude. I did not go with them, because I have first my private wrong to avenge, and I have not yet been able to trace out the valiant captain-of-the-cane, who was the first to fly!'

The old man's face foamed as if he were suffering from an attack of hydrophobia. In his case at least it was not disaffection to the State that had made him what he was. The conduct of the officers in many cases hurried their men into open revolt.

Chapter XV. Enlisted

Shunkur and Probhoo were very much scandalized on hearing the Hávildár's story.

'We blame you not, soldier,' said the first, 'for the position you have assumed. If we understand you aright, you fight both against your personal enemy and against the State. But ours is a grievance of a different kind. We bear the State no grudge.' He then slowly but passionately recounted the story of his wrongs, which even the rude soldier listened to with a moistened eye.

'Unhappy man!' said the Hávildár, 'you have a great wrong indeed to avenge; and though you are not opposed to the State, the prosecution of your private vengeance against two Englishmen can, at this moment, be regarded in no other light than as rebellion against the State; nor will you be able to get at your enemies except in the thickest of the fight. Choose, therefore, whether you will take me with you, or hunt your game apart. You have great responsibilities of your own, and I do not wish to increase them by my company.'

A long private conference between Shunkur and Probhoo was at last terminated by the acceptance of the assistance proffered by the mutineer, and this being settled, it remained now to decide in what direction their campaign was to be opened.

'The state of the case is this, my friends,' said the Hávildár. 'All the country between this and Lucknow is at present in the occupation of the Tálookdárs of Oude and the zemindárs who have risen against the State. These two parties have dissolved their internal strife and dissensions, and have united for the one common object of driving out the English. All of them are collecting large forces of villagers, whom they are arming at their own expense, to co-operate with them. If we believe the enemies we wish to seek out to have proceeded to Lucknow, as I think is most likely, the best thing for us to do would be to take service under one or other of these chiefs, stipulating for our being sent as soon as practicable to fight the British forces at Lucknow. If, on the other hand, we suspect our personal enemies to have gone in any other direction, all we could do at present would be to station ourselves at some centrical place, like Alláhábád, for watching the troops which are constantly passing and repassing it.'

'So far as our men are concerned,' said Shunkur, 'all the information we have been able to collect seems to indicate that they have gone towards Lucknow.'

'I have traced my man also in the same direction,' said the Hávildár, 'and would therefore advise our taking service at once with one of the Oude rájáhs, several of whom are in our immediate neighbourhood, and to be quickly found.'

This was agreed to.

Of the many undeclared rebels of this period one of the best known was Surubdown Sing, the zemindár of Seeáhdee, who carried on his designs with peculiar skill and quite in a systematic manner. He was an old man, but still retained a tall and upright form, with great fire and brilliancy of eyes. It is said that he poisoned one of his wives whom he suspected of unfaithfulness, and killed her son under the conviction that he was a bastard. He was a thorough *budmásh* in other respects also. On the one side he had allied himself with all the rebel chiefs of Oude, and was raising men for their service; on the other hand he was furnishing carriage and supplies to the English commanding-officers, and obtaining certificates of good character from them. A party of fifteen hundred men had just been raised by him for service under Rájáh Bijee Báhádoor Sing, one of the Oude chiefs, and our three volunteers were the last recruits admitted into this band. The men selected were all tall, good-looking soldiers, but ill accoutred and worse armed. They were differently dressed, and while some carried carabines and matchlocks, others were armed only with long lances and *tulwárs*. The leader of this party was one Dabeebux, a large coarse-looking man, who had the reputation of a fearless soldier. Like Náná, he also was known to be inordinately fond of spilling blood; and he made all his recruits swear by Káli and the Korán that no English life, of man, woman, or child, would by any of them be spared. Shunkur and Probhoo took the oath with averted eyes; the Hávildár did so with readiness and alacrity.

'Now let us march on,' said Dabeebux, 'plundering as we go, and slaughtering all whom we may find opposed to us;' and these orders were received by his men with an approving and uproarious shout.

'Ha! what a life we have adopted, my brother,' said Shunkur to Probhoo. 'How many harmless men are destined to suffer death and ignominy at our hands!'

'Regard not the matter in that light, Shunkur,' said Probhoo. 'Remember only the wrongs which have driven us to this course. Providence would not allow us to lead a quiet life. We must move on with the current, as the avenging demons direct us.'

'Yes, as the demons lead us on, and they are hounding us forward to vengeance! But we that have suffered, how can we avoid feeling for those who suffer like us?'

'We must at all events affect not to feel for them. Our comrades are rough soldiers, who must not suspect our feelings, as they are sure to misinterpret them. You need not butcher when they do so; but betray not your detestation for what they do.'

Shunkur made no reply; there was no time for any. They saw before them a small hostile party despatched by the Rájáh of Bánsee, a well-wisher of the English Government, who was determined to oppose the onward movement of Dabeebux. But Dabeebux had the stronger force, and the contest forced on him was quickly decided. The single arm of Dabeebux made terrible havoc among his opponents; and his efforts were ably seconded by several of his followers, notably by the Hávildár. The Bánsee Rájáh's men, finding the affair too hot for them, at last took to their heels, upon which Dabeebux, rearranging his men, pursued his forward course. In rallying his forces, however, he looked at each man with the eye of a chief.

'Our last two recruits,' said he, looking daggers at Probhoo and Shunkur, 'have shown little stomach for the game they have chosen. I shall keep an eye on them, and if I don't find more zeal and earnestness in them hereafter they will have to thank themselves only for what may follow.'

CHAPTER XVI. ONE SIDE OF THE PICTURE

'Pest on these mutineers! 'said Mrs. Carbery, while lolling on her couch in her own palatial residence at Chowringhee; 'they are spreading disaffection throughout India. The storm is closing on us from all sides, and in a short time perhaps Calcutta itself will not be a safe place for us.'

'Is it safe now, my dear?' said her husband, Mr. Patrick Carbery, a Government official in Calcutta of high position, but of tender nerves. 'Who can say to-night what we may have to encounter to-morrow?'

The lady turned pale, and fixed a look of alarm on her husband.

'For shame, Pat!' said Mr. Frederick McGavin, a friend of the family, who had dropped in; 'you have chased away the colour from Mrs. Carbery's face. What on earth have we to fear here, where we are strong enough to eat up all the rebels that the *bazaars* may belch forth?'

'Softly, Bill! It is not simply the rebels that the *bazaars* may give birth to that we have to fear. It is now certain that all the sepoy regiments throughout India are unfaithful to us, and so also are all the great chiefs and zemindárs.'

'I deny both premises *in toto*, Pat,' said McGavin. 'First, as regards the sepoys, without speaking of the armies of Madras and Bombay, it is not just to say even of the army of Bengal that it comprises traitors only, for we know that there are many soldiers in it, and many regiments, that have stood firm against wicked advices and examples, and that at this moment are giving unquestionable proofs of their attachment for us. And as for the landed-gentry, with very few exceptions, it is their interest to side with us, and they have done so. Don't raise a panic, Pat, when there is no reason for any.'

'My dear William, it is blind confidence like yours that has given rise to these disturbances in several places. A little more foresight and prudence on the part of our own officers would have prevented many of the massacres which have been perpetrated by the rebels being so much as attempted with impunity; such, for instance, as those at Bareilly, Jounpore, Fyzábád, and Házáreebágh, leaving out the greater atrocities at Cáwnpore, Delhi, and Meerut altogether. Where were your stanch and true sepoys and zemindárs in those places giving proofs of their unquestionable attachment for us? Attachment! Yes; they have exhibited such attachment as the boa-constrictor shows for the animal it swallows, by first lubricating it with its saliva.'

'Well, the times certainly are out of joint, and you have some reason for your bad opinion, doubtless. The massacres you allude to were particularly atrocious; but instances of faithfulness were not wanting even in the places mentioned.'

'As how? Let us have your version of the events, pray. It will doubtless be of great assistance to the future historian, particularly if he be as sentimental as you are.'

'Well, as to that, I think I am not half so sentimental as I ought to be. The subject is a very serious one. We are traducing a whole nation for the crimes of particular classes only. As for instances of faithfulness, they are too many to be remembered. In Báreilly, Captain Cameron escaped with the assistance of some of his men, and he himself wrote up to the Government that there were thirty other Christians who had been similarly saved by the Hindu inhabitants of Báreilly, Budáon, and Sháhjehánpore. In Jounpore, Mr. Gliddon was sheltered by two natives named Rámprogáus and Hingunláll. At Futtehgurh, Mr. Cumberland and forty other Europeans found protection with a Hindu zemindár named Hurdeo Bux. At Fyzábád, Major Fanthome, his wife, and his daughter found refuge with a Mahomedan chief named Názim Meer Mahomed Khán, who admitted them even into his zenáná for protection!'

'But with what motives?' asked Pat, with a sinister sneer. 'The very men the Názim sent out to rescue the fugitives abused and maltreated them. Had not the wily Mahomedan his own objects to serve?'

'None that casts a stigma on his character. In times so perilous even a chieftain cannot fully control his subordinates; and doubtless the servants of the Názim did maltreat the fugitives so long as they had them in their power. But this ceased the moment they were brought before their chief. He first hid them in his fort, but when that got wind, and an alarm was given that a large party was coming to search for them, the ladies were at once taken into the zenáná, which a Mahomedan holds particularly sacred, and the major was hid in a dark wood-godown, all dressed in the native fashion to insure their security, and it was in this dress that they were quietly conveyed by the Názim's men to the opium factory at Bustee.'

'This certainly was very kind of the Mahomedan,' exclaimed Mrs. Carbery. 'But do you think the story true? I detest these Mahomedans, and am loath to believe that they can be honest.'

'Ah! my good lady, we liked them well enough though before the mutiny broke out. We considered them to be humbler and more respectful than the Hindus, and not less attached to us—'

'Till we were betrayed,' said Carbery, 'and found out our mistake.'

'Then again,' continued McGavin, without heeding the interruption, 'there is the case of the farrier-sergeant Spink, who, escaping from Fyzábád, first found refuge in a village of Bráhmans, where he received needful refreshments. He was thence chased by Bully Sing, a rebel, who dragged him out by the hair from a heap of straw within which he had hid himself, and then marched him on from village to village, with the rabble at his heels hooting at and abusing him. But attachment to us soon appeared in the shape of Thákoor Sing, the brother of Bully Sing, who actually quarrelled with him on behalf of the white man, which led to Spink being saved.'

'Well,' said Carbery, 'there may have been one or two cases of this description, in most of which the poor befriended us, not from any particular attachment to us, but knowing that we always reward the slightest service lavishly.'

'The poor!' exclaimed McGavin; 'in times so hard it is not in the power of the poor to afford much assistance, though they have certainly strained every nerve to do what little they could. We are indebted to all classes for much kindness, which we ought to acknowledge with thankfulness. In Gwálior it was the Rájáh who informed the Political Agent that the whole of the troops (Scindiá's contingent) were disaffected. The wretches had sworn on Ganges water and the Korán to stand by each other, maltreat the English ladies, and kill all Christians, men, women, and children. Did we know anything about it? It was the Rájáh who advised the ladies being sent off to the Residency for protection, and the officers to be prepared for escape. At Hyderábád ten thousand Mahomedans had assembled at a mosque uttering seditious cries, but were put down by Salár Jung and his Arabs. Everywhere, Mrs. Carbery, wherever a European life has been saved, it has been rescued by the natives, be they of high or low degree.'

'They have at least found a good advocate in you, Bill. I dare say you will next contend that it is we that have rebelled against the natives. Eh!'

'That is a large question, and not hurriedly disposed of. We have certainly not treated them as they had a right to be treated by us. But that is not our present thesis. You asked me to cite instances of faithfulness, and I have mentioned such as have occurred to me. In Házáreebágh, and in other places also, the native officers remained steadfast even after their men had risen. "Don't fear, Sáheb," said Subadár Byjenáth Sing to Captain Abbott; "for every drop of water that falls from your eyes they shall shed twenty drops of my blood before any harm shall come to you!"'

'And how was this vaunt justified, Bill? Pray, go on with your illustration.'

'The vaunt was fully justified. "Better service can no man render than this, that he laid down his life for his friend." A short while after the conference the Captain's *kitmutgár* brought word to him that the sepoys were "*biger gyá*", that is, had gone wrong, that they had broken the bell-of-arms and seized their muskets, and that they were running up to murder him. "But where are the officers who promised faithfulness?" Now mark the reply, Pat. "Two of them, Subadár Byjenáth Sing and Jemádár Runjeet Sing, who were running up to tell you, have been seized and are about to be killed. Fly, or we shall be too late."'

CHAPTER XVII. THE OTHER SIDE

'Well, you have had your say, Bill. Now let us see the other side of the picture. You have not alluded to the Cáwnpore massacre at all, nor to the almost equally fearful massacres at Meerut and Delhi: advisedly, I take it; yet the others to which you have referred, differed from them only in the extent of the mischief committed, not in their character. The murder of women and children has been very common everywhere. Many children were dashed to the ground, in Astyanax fashion by the infuriated sepoys; in some villages children's shoes were found with the feet still in them, violently cut off. Barbarities like these brand the character not only of those who were actually guilty of them, but of all others who tolerated them. Even where "attachment" for us has been evinced—I thank you, Bill, for the word—the proportion of avowed rebels to those who were reticent was never less than fifty per cent. At Rohinee the troops did *not* rebel, and yet one officer was killed and two wounded—one of the latter being *scalped* as neatly as any Red Indian could have done it. Kooer Sing, hunted out of Jugdespore, forced his way into the country of a *friendly* rájáh, where he was allowed to hatch further treason with impunity, for all the "attachment" of that other rájáh for us.'

'Stop a bit there, Pat, and take breath. The conspiracy that Kooer Sing did get up in that friendly rájáh's territory did not fructify, simply because he could not get either the rájáh or his relatives (the Thákoors) to back him.'

'Aye, doubtless it was so; for the old foxes were of course too wary to commit themselves. The same story has been repeated in other places in other ways. Chiefs who have been assisting us in escorting our baggages and stores, in collecting carts and transport animals, nay, even in raising forces to fight for us, have also been found to have corresponded with and assisted our enemies; just to keep their bacon safe on both sides of the fire, you know. Father and son have been known to join different sides for the very same reason, which only betrays a villainous method in their "attachment" for us which is particularly edifying.'

'But, my dear Pat, you don't make allowances for their position. The chiefs who corresponded with both parties were in reality perfectly loyal to us. Their conduct was never uncertain, so far as we were concerned, though they were obliged at times to mask it, that is, when they were not able to resist armed men, drilled and disciplined by ourselves, who had made themselves masters of the whole country around them for the time. Was this a crime? They had families of their own to protect from insult, properties to save from spoliation. We, their masters, were utterly impotent to help them. How else could they have acted in such an emergency?'

'Their motives, Bill, are unknown. What they did was perfectly indefensible. It compelled us to hesitate whether we should trust them or not; it encouraged our enemies, who understood their correspondents much better of course than we did.'

'But if we have different reports of their conduct from equally competent authorities,' put in Mrs. Carbery, 'they are entitled to the benefit of the doubt that arises in their favour, are they not, Pat?'

'No, my love. Don't let Bill try to persuade you that they were aught but arrant knaves. It is this principally that makes me so apprehensive of our position; we don't know whom to trust! Besides those who have declared themselves as our enemies, we are surrounded by vast numbers of men who are certainly not friendly to us, who are perhaps now conniving with our avowed enemies, and whom anything—the merest trifle—would induce to join them openly.'

'And who may these be, Pat?' asked Bill.

'Oh! their name is legion. There are the Wáhábees in Pátná; the Ferázees in Dáccá, Furreedpore, and even as near us as Baraset; the Ooriyáhs in Pooree—'

'The Ooriyáhs!' exclaimed McGavin in astonishment. 'Do you really believe that the Ooriyáhs can rise up to fight?'

'Why not? One hundred and fifty-thousand men, more or less, will assemble in Pooree during the Jagganáth festival, and they will have among them those firebrands, the missionaries, who will be preaching to them, in season and out of season, the glad tidings of the Messiah. Where the plea of rebellion is that we are endeavouring to make Christians of all, and to take away their castes, what better pretext can they have than such preaching to declare themselves against us?'

'But I thought the Government had prohibited the missionaries from preaching this season. Is it not so?'

'The Government cannot prohibit preaching. It has appealed to the good sense of the missionaries to avoid putting fire to flax; but will the missionaries listen to the dictates of common sense?'

'Oh me!' cried out Mrs. Carbery in alarm, 'if the Ooriyáhs revolt our Sirdár Bearer here will be murdering us; and there is the Mate Bearer again, who has charge of the children!'

'Never fear, ma'am; the Ooriyáhs will never fight or slay; the Bengalis and the Ooriyráhs, when most aggrieved or in fear, will swamp the Government Secretariats with petitions, and the law-courts with suits for redress. We are quite safe from both these races, are we not, Pat?'

'But who are the others of whom Pat spoke just now?' interrupted Mrs. Carbery; 'who are the Hábábees and the Farábees?'

'Oh, the Wáhábees of Pátná,' said McGavin, 'are a very peculiar brotherhood, of whom the most peculiar feature is their fanatical devotion to their spiritual leaders. The large number and unquestioning submission of their followers make these leaders and the whole sect very dangerous; but up to this time they have not made common cause with the mutineers, and perhaps never will. The understanding among themselves, however, is so perfect, and their fidelity to each other is so stanch, that they could communicate with one another, and take common action together throughout the entire area they inhabit, without any letter being written, or any chance of their conspiracy being detected; and there is no doubt that, if the worst came to the worst, they would not be unwilling to merge all their differences with other Mahomedans, to join in a crusade against us.'

'Oh dear me!' exclaimed Mrs. Carbery, 'why, we sit upon a mine, then, and that prepared for us by those arrant knaves the Mahomedans! Fie, Mr. McGavin! you knew all this, and could speak well of them.'

'I was speaking, ma'am, of the Mutiny, and I only wanted to discriminate between those who were known to be guilty of it and those who were not. Apart from that question, we know of course that the Mahomedans are fanatics, and are at all times ready to deal damnation and the sword to those who do not acknowledge their Prophet.'

'Their Prophet be d—d,' said Mrs. Carbery in irritation; but instantly recollecting herself, she turned round to her husband to ask who the Ferázees were.

'Ask McGavin, my dear. He will best be able to represent his friends. His own delineation of them will best explain what our actual danger is.'

'Well, Mr. McGavin, are these Ferázees also your friends?'

'In one sense, ma'am, they are; that is, since they have kept quiet up to this time. The Ferázee population of Dáccá, Furreedpore, and Baraset are perhaps equally dangerous with the Wáhábees; but they have no leader of note at this moment. The son of their old leader, Teetoo Meáh, exists, and is styled "Sháh Zádá", but he is not a dangerous man. Their other leader, Doodoo Meáh, has suffered under the law. The real head of the sect now in lower Bengal is one Abdool Sobhán, a well-educated and clever man, who preaches weekly to large assemblies. He does not appear to be a man likely to become troublesome, though we don't know, of course, what he would do if the opportunity arose. In the north-west, in Jounpore, there is another party of the Ferázees, which owns the lead of a Moulavi named Kerámut Áli, who is the chief priest of the clan. Of this man we know that he saved two English maidens, the Misses Malcolm, from the mob, and placed them in safety in the fort; so that, so far as our information goes at present, we have nothing to complain of these sects in connection with the mutiny, though, being bigoted Mussulmans, they most undoubtedly detest us cordially.'

'And,' added Carbery, 'are sure to rise if they can find an opportunity to do so.'

'Would it not then be safest for us,' said Mrs. Carbery, 'to remove at once to the shipping for protection? Chowringhee, with its Mahomedan *bustees*, seems scarcely to be a safe place for us now.'

CHAPTER XVIII. A MURDER, AND A RECRUIT

A drive of ten minutes from Chowringhee would bring the reader to the black-town of Calcutta, where, in the magnificent residence of the De Mullicks, in one of the dirtiest streets of the metropolis, an angry son was plotting the death of his own father, while the whole country around him was passing through the throes of a convulsion. The hour was past midnight, and the house was hushed and dark, except that one small room was faintly lighted by a native *chirág*. The apartment was not well furnished, though there were several articles of costliness and luxury scattered about it. Its only occupant was the young man referred to, whose ill-regulated mind appeared to have been recently disturbed in an unwonted degree by some disagreement with his father, and on whose features the fatal sign of inordinate anger was still struggling visibly.

There was a slight tap at the door at this moment.

'Did master call?' was the simple query of the man who entered.

'Ah! Did I call you, Ojáh? answered De Mullick. 'It must have been so, then; but my passions are beyond my mastery now, and I know not what I called you for.'

'Master seems much vexed and wounded,' returned the servant. 'Master's eyes are glaring wildly. If there be any difficulty that I can remove, master may always command me.'

'Mock me not,' said the young man hurriedly. 'What service canst thou render me in my present difficulty? I feel the old man like a thorn at my side. I cannot remove that thorn; can you?' The voice of the young man trembled as he spoke, and his last words sank into a scarcely audible whisper.

'I can,' was Ojáh's firm reply; but young De Mullick seemed staggered by its very briefness. He cast a hurried look around him, and with a trembling hand pulled out a well-filled purse.

'There, there! Don't hurt him; that is not what I mean. This will be doubled to you every year as long as I live.'

Ojáh took the gold, but gave no reply. Two days after the senior De Mullick was waylaid and murdered, in an obscure alley of a petty village, by a masked man who was hotly pursued, but never taken. His son received the news as a pistol-shot through the heart. His dizzy brain swam and reeled, and he was never seen to smile again. Friends and neighbours pitied him that he felt his loss so severely; but other faces peered on him less kindly in the dark, and he heard other sounds that chased slumber from his eyes.

Large rewards were offered for the apprehension of the murderer, many surmises thrown out of his motive for the crime, and the myrmidons of the police actively engaged for a long time in unravelling the mystery; but all to no purpose, the enigma was never explained. A *Sunnyási*, who a few days after passed out of the village where the crime was perpetrated, was traced from temple to temple, almost all over Bengal, till all clue of him was lost on the way to Lucknow. Was he killed by the mutineers, or did he die red-handed fighting against the English? Who can tell!

'A strange-looking man,' said Gungádeen to Dabeebux, 'has been hanging on our rear for the past few days; he is perhaps a spy of Mán Sing. Shall we send him to his last account?'

'Not in a hurry. First get hold of him. Your roving blades make good recruits, and perhaps he may be of service to us.'

The man was captured, and, though of great personal strength, did not resist.

'Who and what are you?'

'A soldier, and in want of service.'

'A soldier! To what regiment did you belong?'

'That does not matter. I am able-bodied, and can give a soldier's service.'

'But it does concern us to know whom we enlist.'

'My name is Sáhebrám, and I come from Behár.'

'Have you nothing further to mention?'

'Nothing, but that I am in want, and will take any service.'

'Ah! physical want to a man of your size is a portentous evil, and we are willing indeed to relieve it. But our position makes us suspicious. We cannot take into our service every vagabond we come across, lest we be betrayed.'

'Betrayed? To whom? If you mean the British Government and their partisans, I have even greater reason to fear them than you have.'

'That will do,' said Dabeebux; 'we have lived long enough in the world to understand each other now. Let him be enlisted, and the usual oath administered.'

Sáhebrám had really been a soldier at one time of his life—a bold soldier, but a bolder villain. He had, however, the trick of making friends; his conversation was unshackled and free, but never repellent; and he soon made friends, not only with the Hávildár, but also with Shunkur and Probhoo.

'Revenge! Revenge is a feast for the gods,' said he; 'and I would gladly share your dangers, and help you in obtaining it, if you will allow me.'

'Fully and cordially,' was Shunkur's reply. And so the four became sworn friends.

Chapter XIX. Before Lucknow, and Away From It

The enemy were in immense force at Lucknow, and the works round the city were really formidable. All the great chiefs—Mussulman and Hindu—had sworn to fight for young Birjis Kádder to the last. The great bulk of the sepoy army was there, and the army of the king was not undisciplined. Over and above all this was the Begum, a woman of great energy and ability, ardent, intriguing, and passionately devoted to the cause of her son.

The English in Lucknow had lost everything but two positions, namely, the Residency and Munchee Bhowán; but several detachments were coming to their rescue from different directions. Sir James Outram's forces were the first to arrive, but soon found themselves in as bad straits as those whom they had come to relieve. It was not till General Havelock joined them that any well-founded hopes of success were entertained.

It would be beyond our purpose to notice here all the hard fighting that occurred. Both the mutineers and the king's army fought well; but the joint attacks of Outram and Havelock, from two distinct positions, were more than they could withstand. The Begum, still undismayed, encouraged her followers with a smiling face, and they, though fully satisfied that they were losing ground, fought on with unabated zeal, dying sword in hand in the streets.

Of the many bands that fought so resolutely one of the stanchest was that commanded by Dabeebux.

'They run, they run!' cried Gungádeen, when he saw one of the parties they were opposed to give way.

'Press on them and cut them down,' said Dabeebux. 'Brave Hávildár, and you, Shunkur, Probhoo, and Sáhebrám, press on. Well have you earned the glory of this day.'

The feint of the English detachment was, however, not ineffective. They had wished and succeeded in drawing off a great body of the besieging force from before the Residency; after which they effected their retreat in excellent order, while their undisciplined opponents were dispersed in different directions. Dabeebux kept together his men as well as he could, and, hearing that Náná Sáheb was hard beset in the jungle-fort of Churdá, he went off in that direction to aid him. This move was suggested by the Hávildár, who had traced his captain-of-the-cane among those in pursuit of the hero of Bithoor; but it was a long time before the party could come up to Náná, as he was constantly changing his position. Many stray detachments of English soldiers were met with on the way. Dabeebux did not always encounter them face to face; he preferred to hang on their rear and harass them: and his movements were so well-timed that he gave them no rest.

It was about noon on a moist day in August that they came up to the bank of a rivulet, or *nulláh*, in the neighbourhood of Nánpáráh, within a short distance of the position occupied by Náná Sáheb. In front of them was a small body of British troops, rather strongly posted, and protected by guns in position; but the rebels were in greater strength, and understood their advantage, and, directing their attack with pluck and ability, were soon in the midst of their adversaries. The onset was maintained with great courage, and though the English guns returned the enemy's fire briskly, the English detachment was compelled to break ground. Flushed with their success, the rebels pressed on, while the English, keeping up a running fight, fell back towards a dense jungle that afforded them a safe retreat. The loss among them was comparatively heavy, and night only put a stop to the fight.

On arriving at the base of one of the jungle-slopes Sáhebrám saw a man hiding behind a bush. He told him to come out, but no reply being received, he called Shunkur and the Hávildár, and all three went forward to capture the skulker. Sáhebrám seized the man's musket when he was just on the point of full-cocking it, after which he was easily taken. He begged hard for mercy, and Shunkur was for granting it, when Probhoo, having come up, recognised him as the wretch Mackenzie, one of the two miscreants they had been looking after so long. No words were now wasted; he was deliberately stabbed to the heart by the brother of his victim.

'Oh, my poor sister!' exclaimed Probhoo, 'thy wrongs can never be fully avenged; but this is all that we can do to vindicate thy worth:' and he then hung the corse on a tree for kites to peck at.

'One villain is now disposed of,' said Shunkur; 'we have another yet to find out.'

'Not so,' said the Hávildár; 'there remain two still to hunt for. That was the bargain, friends, we made.'

'Two more surely,' said Probhoo, 'before our work is done.'

'Is it so?' exclaimed Sáhebrám. 'But my work, when and how will that terminate?'

CHAPTER XX. TIT FOR TAT

General Neill had now taken command at Cáwnpore, and was proving how heroically the English could repay the cowardly brutality of the rebels and mutineers.

'Whenever a rebel is caught,' said he, 'we shall try him and hang him at once if he cannot prove a defence. But the chief rebels and ringleaders—they shall first clean the blood they have shed, and then pay the penalty of their crimes.'

This vigour was much lauded by the local English papers and community of the day. 'The word "Mercy",' said the Rev. Dr. Bluff, 'was never intended to be made applicable to fiends.' 'The Bible,' remarked the amiable editor of the *Hurryrámpore Weekly,* 'expressly says that Canaan is cursed and doomed to be a servant of servants; also that the children of Japheth were born to rule over those of Shem.' It was in vain that one or two learned missionaries pointed out that the Bible was being misquoted and misrepresented; that the revengeful and relentless feelings displayed were utterly unchristian and unjustifiable. The display of vigour had come into fashion, and no homily had any chance of being listened to.

'Three prisoners to-day, sir!' reports Corporal Quinn; 'one a Mahomedan, one a Hindu of substance, and the third a sepoy.'

'Hang them all on the nearest tree,' replies the commanding-officer. 'The Mahomedan must be a traitor; the Hindu, since he has substance, must have acquired it unfairly; and the sepoy is necessarily a mutineer.'

Two Mahomedans were shot because they had scowled on Lieutenants

Taperley and Smogton, who had merely set fire to their huts; and the punishment was justified by the verdict of a court of inquiry. Villages were burnt without any precautions being taken to rescue the women and children from the common destruction, lest such leniency should be misunderstood. Miss Jemima and Miss Fitzbuggins shook their pretty little fists at manacled sepoys, and called them 'niggers,' and officers dressed in scarlet and gold applauded them for doing so. The angry Britons not only fought with the sepoys, but also with Coolies and Khánsámás, nay, even with Mathránis—so they were ill-looking. Rájáh Binodilálĺ's house was searched, and a large booty collected, for he was a rich man, and had an immense quantity of gold, silver, and shawls. Was he not a traitor? The man was so ill-favoured that he could not possibly be otherwise. He protested against the inference, and no arms or munitions of war were found in his house. But lo! among some papers was found a prayer addressed to Mahádeva, beseeching him to assist the devotee in the destruction of Europeans! Was not this enough? The man disclaimed all knowledge of the paper, and pointed to the folly of supposing that even a traitor should write such an effusion at such a time and leave it so exposed to be cited against himself. Stuff! British soldiers were not going to stand such nonsense! The rájáh was strung up, and the booty partitioned! Irádut Jehán and Fasáhut Jehán, two obstinate rebels, gave great trouble before they were caught and hung. To strike salutary terror among all similar miscreants their women were given up to the soldiers, and many of them died of the injuries they received!

'Is Rám Sing stanch and true? It looks suspicious, for he was seen to have joined the Oude insurgents on one occasion.'

'Oh, there is no doubt about him; he is true as steel,' was the reply. 'He only joined the Oude men on hearing that, the rebels having been defeated, the British forces were about to disgrace the seraglio of the Nawáb. He had eaten the Nawáb's salt, and marched to protect the women.'

Be it so; the question did not admit of careful sifting.

This at least was certain, that it was not expedient to doubt Rám Sing's fidelity, and see his strength and influence enlisted on the wrong side!

'Who was it? Was it not Captain Ahern who, having taken the fortress of Meetágurh, ordered all the garrison, including the sick and the infirm to be hung, and all the people of the neighbourhood to be cut down!'

'Yes; prompt and decisive measures were necessary, and he did not hesitate. A brave soldier was Ahern, his country's pride. "Revenge on the miscreants!" was his war-cry, and he did his work well.'

The judgments of heaven are usually slow; but in the case of the Indian Mutiny they were unusually quick and vigorous. Why does Britannia look brooding and sorrowful? Does she regret all that was done in her name?

CHAPTER XXI. NÁNÁ'S FLIGHT, AND SHUNKUR'S REVENGE

Náná has been compelled to retreat before his enemies, and is approaching the confines of Nepál. The snowy range rises before him, and intermediately on the slopes of the mountains are forests of untold depths inhabited by tigers, in which man has never set foot. In the ravines formed by the course of innumerable torrents are paths unknown except to a few; but these are yet destined to be trodden by many who in their dream of dreams had never anticipated such fate.

'Death is better than this suspense,' said Náná, 'and I shall throw myself before the first tiger I come across; for in my present condition it will be a satisfaction even to be torn up by a wild beast.'

'You shall not do so, my love,' said his good and faithful wife. 'Am I not with you, and must you not protect and cherish me?'

Náná spoke not. Oh! for the love of woman, has it anything equal to it in life? Náná clasped his wife to his heart, and they were happy—happy in the hollows and gaps of the mountains within which they were crouching like hares—happier in their concealment within the long jungle-grass than they had ever been in the palace of Bithoor.

But they were hard beset. A few adherents still remained with them, but their demeanour towards them had already become cold. The enemies behind them were stronger and more alert; but they had, fortunately for the fugitives, no one to guide them through the ravines.

'Hush! who is that? Captain Neville, is it you?'

'Yes, Bernard. But how is it that you have groped through your way hither?'

'Ah, the same talisman has drawn us both. Náná's life is worth his weight in gold.'

'But who shall have the gold, then; you or I?'

'We shall divide it between us, my boy; let us help each other.'

'Ha! Divide the reward, and with thee, when I have hunted my game so far alone? No, Bernard, you are a blockhead to think of it! Go back from the pursuit, or I shall settle the difficulty with you here.'

'Why, you provoking fool, how over-hot you are! Are you so sure of capturing the Náná alone that you refuse to receive my assistance on the only terms I could offer it? Náná has arms, and knows how to use them.'

'He has arms to use against cowards. But that is neither here nor there. Will you go back or not?'

'But I cannot, Neville, really I cannot, because I don't know my way. I have quietly groped up after you. How can I got back alone?'

'By heavens! you madden me. If you remain with me I will stab you to the heart.'

'No, you must not. I will stay with you to assist you, if you want my help, but not to advance any claim on your reward.'

'Swear!'

'I do.' And he repeated after Neville the oath that the latter dictated to him.

'But they are two there, I see. It is fortunate, Neville, that I came.'

'Hush! don't speak loud. They are only man and wife.'

'Wife! Nána's wife, and in the Terái?'

'Yes.'

'Then we can yet divide the prize. You take Nána; I, his wife.'

'What will you do with her?'

'Oh, never mind that. Do you agree to give her up to me?'

'I do; for I don't want her myself.'

It was quite dark, and no assistance was near; and simultaneously Nána and his wife felt the strong grasp by which each was held down. A faint shriek burst forth from the lips of the latter; while the former, drawing out his dagger, used it with better effect. The stroke was well-aimed, and Captain Neville let go his hold, upon which Nána ran forward, and was lost in the intricacies of deeper jungles and ravines. In the meantime his wife screamed loudly in the arms of Bernard, till he stunned her by a blow. But the consummation of further wickedness was prevented by the arrival of the assistance the lady's cries had called up; and in the next moment Bernard was struggling within the strong grasp of Shunkur, from which he never came out alive.

'Again at your old crime, caitiff? Was not one victim enough?'

'Let go my windpipe, knave. Wherefore wilt thou murder me?'

'Is thy victim of Soorájpore forgotten? Behold her husband and avenger in me! The prince of Bithoor may be unmindful of his wife; but the poor clown of Soorájpore knows how to avenge the woman who had lain by his side.' A wild gleam of satisfaction shot across the features of the avenger, his hold on Bernard's necktie was tightened, and the next moment that villain was a corse.

'Save me! hide me!' cried the wife of Nána, startled from her swoon.

'I will, lady, since I have been so fortunate as to rescue thee.'

Very opportunely had Shunkur arrived at the spot; but he had not come alone. Sáhebrám, Probhoo, the Hávildár, and Shunkur had, all four, detached themselves from the bulk of their party with the especial object of coming up to the personal assistance of Nána Sáheb, and it was after fighting dreadful odds that they were able to approach him. Leaving Bernard in Shunkur's grasp, Sáhebrám had pushed on after Nána himself, and neither was seen again, both probably having proceeded on to Nepál, though it was never known for certain that they reached it. The Hávildár's attention was first drawn to Captain Neville, whom he recognised at once as his captain-of-the cane. But Náná's stab had settled his long account, and seeing that nothing now remained for him to do, the Hávildár determined to follow in Náná's wake, as he had no hopes of protection on English ground.

'Oh! take me with thee, good old man,' cried out Náná's wife; 'take me to my husband. I also have no home or refuge in India; and if I prove a burden to thee on the way, kill me, and leave my body on the roadside for the wild animals to feed upon. Even that is better than that I should fall into the hands of such enemies as he from whom thy comrade has delivered me.'

'Yes, lady; the course you have chosen is the best for you. I shall take care of you as if you were my own child; and, if any can, I shall be able to replace you by the side of your husband.'

'And we,' said Probhoo, who had just come up, 'whither shall we go after all we have done?'

'Return to your home at Soorájpore,' said the Hávildár, 'to the old mother and little boy you have left behind. Forget your connection with these bloody doings, and no one else will remember them against you.'

'The Hávildár speaks well,' said Shunkur. 'There is no further motive for the life we were obliged to adopt: let us go back to our cheerless home.'

The Street-Music of Calcutta

[By Shoshee Chunder Dutt. From *Bengaliana: A dish of Rice and Curry, and Other Indigestible Ingredients*.]

I devoted a whole day to listen to the street-music of Calcutta, and report the result for the information of my readers. The cries to which I refer are to be heard daily in the native part of the town. Those peculiar to the European portion of it are of course very different.

I. KOOAR-GHOTEE-TOLLÁH![23]

Almost the first cry every morning is that of the *Kooar-ghotee-tolláh*. Be the day ever so cold or so rainy there is the man ready to extricate from the bottom of the well whatever you may have dropt in it, though the cry speaks of brass *lotahs* only. The Moorish lady[24] cried her heart out for the earrings she had dropt in the well, which she could not recover. There must have been no *kooar-ghotee-tolláh* in Spain in her day, for earrings, or nose-rings, or finger-rings, are all picked out of wells in Calcutta with the greatest facility. Look at the man as he stands before you—an elderly, stout fellow, with elephantiasis on one leg—and you would hardly think him capable of the feat by which he earns his daily bread. He must dive at least five or six times a day to earn a decent pittance, for two or three pice is all he gets each time; and the frail steps on the well-side by which he gets down are not contemptible dangers to brave for the price paid to him. Talk of old Bazaine's escape from Fort St Marguerite![25] It surely was not half so perilous as these incessant descents into wells kept as dirty as can be imagined and in indifferent repair; and yet who has ever heard of a *ghotee-tolláh* having died in the execution of his duty?

But have not water-pipes superseded the use of wells in every family-residence in Calcutta? asks the English reader, entirely innocent of native ways and doings. No, Aryan brother, they have not. The supply of Municipal water is little to be depended upon, and fails frequently at very inconvenient hours; and our Hindu ladies are so aquatic in their habits, and delight so much in water, that an unfailing supply of it from 4 a.m. to 10 p.m. is an absolute necessity of their lives. Almost every act of housewifery requires the washing of hands or clothes, and many make entire ablutions of the body imperative; and since the filtered water of the Municipality is not to be had at all hours, there is no alternative for the mass but the well and the *ghotee*. They speak again, of the compulsory setting-up of metres in private houses to regulate the supply of water according to the rate paid for it. The idea is not particularly liberal; to our thinking the supply of water, like that of air and light, should be unchecked. But, as our sapient commissioners seem to think otherwise, 'don't fill up your wells yet' is our warning and advice to all whom it may concern.

II. THE SONG OF THE MÁKHUM CHORÁ[26]

This is a song of the boyhood of Krishna, when that mischievous urchin used to go about from dairy to dairy stealing butter. The itinerant singer goes, Homer-like, from house to house, singing the delinquencies of the little god, that the morning might be commenced auspiciously by all, with the achievements of the deity fresh in their recollections. It is rather odd giving lessons in thieving to business-people at this early hour, as the instruction is not unapt to stick in the minds of those who buy and sell, and to influence their actions throughout the day. Songs about Rámchandra are also sung. For these regular reminders the singers claim a small *buxis* (varying from four pice to two annas) at the end of each month. The songs are good to hear, and some of the singers have very musical voices; and so, for one reason or another, the imposition is tolerated by all families.

III. JYE RÁDHAY! BHIKAYÁPYE BÁBÁ?[27]

The begging appeals in Calcutta are intolerable nuisances that recur from daybreak to dusk; and there is no means of putting them down, as the police will *never* interfere. I don't object to an old woman, or a blind or lame man, appealing to one for charity; but for two real objects of sympathy that accost you, there are four or six stalwart claimants whose only plea for appeal is that they are Vysnubs, which they think gives them a right to *demand* alms. They actually give you *gállee* if you send them away empty-handed. 'What, such a Burrá Báboo, with such a house to live in, and not give alms! Remember there is another place to go to; for he that turns away the beggar from his door gets no admittance in Vycant.' Cheek of this sort is constantly given; and as you can't condescend to resent it, you are obliged to submit to it with the best grace you can. Often, very often, a sturdy beggar will refuse to leave your door without a reasonable dole. If you ask the *páháráwállá* to eject him, the man of authority laughs at your face; if you tell your own people to push out the applicant, there is an action for assault, sometimes resulting in a fine: at all events, I remember having once read of such a case, in which the learned magistrate held that force should not have been used for expulsion, without laying down however how the expulsion was otherwise to be effected when the party to be dealt with is strong-limbed, obstinate, and clamorous.

Of course, as I have said, there are many real objects of charity, who, in a city where there is absolutely no provision for them, well deserve the attention of the humane. But, when your temper is once upset by stubbornness, it rarely happens that you are able to do your duty to the rest. 'Don't admit any of them,' is the snappish order the master gives to his door-keeper; and so many a poor woman loses the pice or grain that she would otherwise have received.

IV. SISSEE, BOTTOLE BIKREE![28]

This is an expressive cry, a proof of the march of civilization as represented by the brandy-bottle. From house to house the *Bikreewállá* collects all the empty bottles, in broad daylight, as a matter of course, and without any attempt whatever at concealment. The cry is constantly raised that Young Bengal is afraid to avow his liberalism; but surely the avowal, as regards the consumption of spirituous liquors, is distinct enough. *Sissees* (medicine phials) are, of course, also asked for; but you see every *Bikreewállá* passing by loaded with champagne, beer, and brandy bottles, with their labels on. It is an every-day and every-hour matter now, and the number of *Bikreewállás* is so large that one is staggered in attempting to compute the amount of consumption it represents. If you detect me in giving out bottles from my house, I have my answer ready: 'Some rose-water bottles only, which I do not know what to do with. But pray, don't smell them; bad gases may have generated in them, and you may fare the worse for doing so.'

V. POORÁNÁ KÁGOCH![29]

What a stentorian voice that bearded Mahomedan has who every morning cries out at your door for old newspapers! Do the worthy gents of the fourth estate know what their bad grammar and worse taste actually sell for second-hand in the Calcutta *bazaárs*? Fourteen pice the quire; not a cowrie more! I haggled very hard once for 4 annas; but the devout Mahomedan swore by Álláh Bismalláh that he barely gets that rate from the shopkeepers, and could not therefore give me more than the fixed $3\frac{1}{2}$ annas a quire. Twenty-four sheets of an *Indian Thunderer* for fourteen pice only! With this data given, will any B.A. or M.A. work out for us how much each furious leader is appraised at? I am not a dab at figures, but my calculations give just $9\frac{1}{2}$ cowries for the biggest thunder—English or Patriotic. Some of these thunder-

makers have sought sedulously for immortality by having blind-lanes named
after them. The immortality of the whole genus will be found in the shops of
the *Pánchunwálláhs*, if they will only seek for it there.

Akin to the above cry are the cries of

VI. POORÁNÁ LOHÁ BIKREE![30]
VII. POORÁNÁ CHÁTTÁ BIKREE![31]
VIII. POORÁNÁ NAKRÁ KÁNI BIKREE![32]

There is no such thing as destruction in the world, says the philosopher.
What we consider as such is only change. Your old iron, your old *cháttá* or
parasol, all your tattered rags, are marketable articles: there is no destruction
for them, but a salutary change? The broken padlock will do service again in
another shape; the *cháttá* will receive a new era of existence after it is mended
and a new cloth put on to it; the rags will be converted into paper—probably
to print some big daily, to be sold again at $3^1/2$ annas a quire! O tempora! O
mores!

IX. DHONG! DHONG! DHONG!

There goes the Kánsári's music! A cooly carries with him all the articles he has
for sale. The gong and the bell are for *poojáhs*, if you are particularly fond of
them; the *thállá*, or dining plate, for your first-born, if he has commenced to
eat rice; the *lotáh*, the *pilsooj*, the *gároo*, anything you stand in need of, sir!
But I don't want anything; still the infernal *dhong! dhong!* continues. It is
enough to awaken the dead in their graves!

The Kánsári is a man well to do in life. He has a shop in the nearest *bazaár*;
and both in going to it and in coming back from it he makes it a point to
carry a cooly's load with him, if only to try the temper of the people whose
houses he passes by. Braziers from other places, especially from Jagganáth,
also frequent the streets, crying, *Thákoorbáteer bássan go! Thákoobáteer bássan!*
But this you don't hear every day, probably because the sellers are few in
number, and perambulate different parts of the town by turns.

X. KÁTÁO SEEL-CHÁKTEE, JÁNTÁ![33]

This is a horrible voice between a bawl and a screech. I wonder how much
the man makes a day by this cry. Who on earth requires grinding-stones to
be recut and repaired? And yet here is a man who makes his living by cutting
them anew.

XI. BHÁLO, BHÁLO, NAYÁ, NAYÁ, SÁP; SÁPAY BÁNDORAY
TAMÁSHÁR KHAYLE[34]

Here is poetry for you, reader; the serpent-charmer's poetry, as he goes about with his baskets full of serpents, a baboon following at his heels that will play many tricks with the serpents, if you will pay a trifle for the *tamáshá*. It is, of course, well-known that the serpents are fangless; but what if one of the reptiles escapes while being played with and burrows in your house? Won't it get new fangs in time? Why then is the play permitted in a densely-crowded city? I never could look at serpents without dread. Our native dress at home gives us no protection against them if they are unwarily crossed and I would unhesitatingly vote for the expulsion of all such players from the town. I know that there are many who take a delight in looking at the reptiles— particularly children. The impression left on these little fellows is various. One child, after such a sight in the day, woke up at night in convulsions, with the cry of 'Sáp,' 'Sáp,' and with froth foaming in his mouth. But this was an exceptional case. Generally, they are well pleased with the play so long as it lasts, and forget all about it afterwards; what especially delights them being the music of the charmer, which certainly does charm all simple-hearted listeners—including the serpents, of course. These charmers, they say, can charm out serpents from their holes and capture them. I saw one attempt myself, but that was a failure. The serpent did come out to listen to the music, but snapped at the charmer every time that he approached it; and, as it was a rather large-sized cobra, the man did not much like the idea of cultivating any intimate acquaintance with it. But there is no doubt that they do capture many serpents in this way, for many good people have seen them do so.

XII. CHYE MOONG-KE-DÁL?[35]

A very good edible is *Moong-ke-dál*, the Arabicá Revelentá of the doctors, which has been known in this country from time anterior to the flood as a very wholesome food for the convalescent. The man who sells the *dál* is an up-country man, and the grains are very clean and have been well picked. The Bengali does not know, or does not care, to clean his grains in the way these up-country people do it. The fact is he is more partial to his fish and *torkáree* than to his *dál*, though the *dál* is both more wholesome and more strengthening. Altogether, in the matter of food, the natives of Bengal are very much less particular than up-country Hindus. The former will take anything they can get that caste rules allow, and then hurry on to money-making; while the latter, though not less fond of money-making, will still find full time for cleaning and cooking their dinner well.

XIII. HÁNSAYR DEEM CHYE; HÁNSAYR DEEM, GO! HÁNSAYR DEEM![36]

How loud the man bawls! His custom perhaps is not as profitable as it used to be of old. Young Bengal is more fond of *Moorgeer Deem* (fowls' eggs) than of *Hánsayr Deem* (ducks' eggs); but of course the former cannot be hawked about openly except in Mahomedan quarters. The *Hánsayr Deem* is a loathsome food. Of fowls' eggs I have no personal experience, but they are said to be better. Both are taken by some people raw!!! and I have heard that doctors advise their being so taken. The idea makes the blood run cold.

XIV. BELÁTEE ÁMRÁ CHYE; CHYE PÁT-BÁDÁM![37]
XV. ÁLOO CHYE; PIÁZ CHYE?[38]

The first may pass without comment; but *Áloo* (potatoes) and *Piáz* (onions) selling together in the streets of an orthodox town! Oh Menu and Vyasa![39] what are we coming to? There was a time when people lost caste for eating onions; while now potatoes and onions are carried round in the same basket from door to door, and even widows and Bráhmans buy the potatoes quite heedless of their unorthodox contamination.

XVI. CHYE MÁLSEE DOHI; MÁLSEE DOHI CHYE, GO![40]

The cry is drawn out in lengthened sweetness, and reaches a great distance; and very great is the demand for the *dohi*. All people who can afford to pay for it buy it eagerly, for it very much facilitates the taking of rice—particularly when the days are hot. It is also very wholesome, notwithstanding some medical opinions expressed of late to the contrary. In bowel complaints it acts as a charm. The other variety of it, called *Málye Dohi*, is less digestible, and is only liked because it is more acid. They both sell in the streets with the greatest promptitude.

XVII. TOOK-TÁP, TOOK-TOOM

Play-things to sell! What a crowd of ragged children follow in the wake of the seller; all anxious to buy, but having no pice to pay! And what a variety of nicknacks the man has got; birds made of coloured rags and decked with tinsel, paper *pálkees, gharries*, umbrellas, trees flowers, whistles, bells, cards, balloons, looking-glasses; everything, in fact, that is likely to catch a child's fancy. With villainous pertinacity these are displayed ostentatiously at every door. In vain do poor mothers tell the man to pass on, not having the pice to pay for what their children clamorously ask for. The man knows that the pice will be forthcoming, and generally succeeds in getting it out.

XVIII. CHOOREE LIBEE, GO![41]

What a sweet melodious voice that girl has who goes from house to house selling *choorees*, or bracelets made of sealing-wax or glass! But all the poetry evoked by her voice vanishes the moment you get a full view of her face. The phiz of Medusa could scarcely have had a more petrifying effect. You close your eyes involuntarily, while the ear continues to drink the melody that floats by. *Chooree libee, go!* Yes, my love, I will buy up all your *choorees* if you will go on hawking them in your own pretty way; but don't break the spell by turning your face towards me, or you will convert me into stone. Throw a veil over your features, and you will enhance the value of your wares.

XIX. GHOTEE BÁTEE SÁRÁBAY! GHORÁ, PILSOOJ SÁRTAY ÁCHYA! BHÁNGÁBÁSUN SÁRTAY ÁCHAY![42]

No, man, no! I have no broken utensils to repair; pass on, please; your pertinacity is most annoying. Who can possibly require a tinker at his door every day of the year?

XX. RIPOOR KORMO![43]
XXI. SALIE JOOTEÁ; JOOTÁ BROOSH![44]
XXII. DO GOLIE SOOTÁ EK PYSÁ![45]
XXIII. DHÁMÁ BÁNDÁBAY, GO![46]
XXIV. BÁXO SÁRTAY ÁCHAY?[47]

These shrieks and screeches are very trying indeed. There is no poetry in the voices. They are all matter-of-fact calls, for things or services which you cannot possibly stand in need of more than, say, once, twice, or four times a year; and yet you have to bear with the calls every blessed day of your existence, and fortunate is he who does not receive each more than once in twenty-four hours.

XXV. JÁRUCK LABOO, BELMOROBÁ, HUZMEE GOLEE, ÁMBÁCHÁR, TOPÁCOOL, KÁSUNDI![48]

A good long yarn this, and rather melodiously bawled out, hawking for sale *chutnies* and acids which are dear to every epicure and gourmand.

XXVI. MONDÁ, METOY![49]
XXVII. ROOTEE, BISKOOT, NÁNKHÁTÁYE![50]
XXVIII. GOLÁPEE AOOREE CHYE?[51]
XXIX. CHYE NAKOLE DÁNÁ?[52]

We pass over all these cries as calling for no particular remark.
Immediately after them follows the cry of

XXX. CHÁNÁCHOOR GURMÁ-GURRUM[53]

Your *syce* is a great scoundrel and steals gram; the horse is getting thinner; you are afraid of being some day hauled up before the Magistrate by the Cruelty-Prevention-Society, which is so vigilant. But where the deuce does the gram go to? Ask this man and you will know. All the stolen gram is converted into *Chánáchoor*, which, made hot with chillies, is much valued by drunkards both of high and low degree. *Brandy-páwny* and *Chánáchoor Gurmá-Gurrum* comprise a feast for the gods, leaving aside the exquisites of the Calcutta University. What Young Bengal is there who has been able to resist the temptation of sharing them with his *syce* or his *sirdár-bearer*, if not in worse company?

XXXI. CHYE BUROPH?

And there is the *Burophwállá* coming in good time to cool down both the liquid-fire and chillied-gram! Does any one wish to have revelations of pandemonium or the purgatory without the intervention of the Planchette? Let him accompany a *Burophwállá* for the nonce, and he will see both places with his open eyes and learn all that he may require to know. Oh, what secrets these *Burophwállás* could divulge if they had a mind to!

Night now closes up the city of palaces, brothels, and iniquities for a brief while; and no calls but those of the *Páháráwállá* and the jackal will be heard for the next few hours. I may therefore close for the present with—

XXXII. YÁPEED MOOSHKILLÁSHÁN KARAYGÁ,[54]

Which is announced by a broad flaring light in the hands of a bearded *fakir*, who goes about from door to door, asking for that dole in the name of a Mahomedan saint which no Hindu housewife dares to refuse. All *Mooshkill*, or difficulties, will be made *áshán*, or easy. Child's sickness, husband's irregularity of life, crustiness of old mother-in-law—every impediment to happiness will be removed at once. And what is the price to pay for this? One pice only!

The Republic of Orissá;
A Page from the Annals of the Twentieth Century

[By Shoshee Chunder Dutt. From *Bengaliana: A dish of Rice and Curry, and Other Indigestible Ingredients.*]

The republic of Orissá was comprised, till a recent period, within the dominions of the British Crown, and extended from the confines of Bengal on the north, to those of the Circárs on the south. Berár formed its western boundary, and the Bay of Bengal washed it on the east. But the boundaries of the new republic have been, by an Act of its Congress, passed in the year of Christ 1925, extended in a western and southern direction over a considerable portion of Berár, and to the whole of the Circárs. On the east, also, it has increased its empire over the alluvial land left by the retreating waters of the sea.

This delightful country, some seventy years ago, was inhabited by a weak and niggard race of aborigines, some scores of white settlers, a few Asiatic foreigners, and a horde of wild animals. But, year after year, since the earthquake of 1899, which is supposed by the superstitious nations of Europe to have effected a complete change in the constitution of the world, the enormous herds of the wilderness have been swept away with resistless rapidity, making room for wilder and more fearful denizens—untamed men. Amongst the various tribes that roam over the interior of Orissá, the name of the Kingáries, or hill-tribes, has long been the most terrible to the neighbouring powers. The preeminence of these tribes is not only secured by their superiority in numbers, but by a combination of great physical strength with an intrepidity and courage unknown to any other people of the world. They stray in large predatory bands, pillaging without distinction all whose unguarded attitude tempts their cupidity. Their chief arms are battle-axes and spears; but the deadly use of a Nágpore rifle is not unknown to them. However the name of these tribes may be connected with cruelty, robbery, and blood-shed, still it is one which is emblazoned on the triumphant flag of freedom; for Orissá owes her liberty to the daring adventures of her Kingáries.

On the 25th June, of the year 1916, was passed, in the Council Chamber at Pillibheet (the capital of British India), an Act, permitting a system of oppression revolting to the refined ideas of the Indian public. The purport of it was, that, it being found cheaper to support Indian labourers as slaves than to employ them at fixed wages, slavery was from that time forward to be re-established in British India, against all provisions to the contrary. And the Act stated—

1.That the title to a slave was established by its being proved that he or she was the issue of parents known and acknowledged to be Hindus by birth, and had voluntarily sold his or her freedom, or had his or her freedom sold by such parents.

2. That parents had a right to sell their children, and all children thus sold were to be considered as slaves.

3. That slaves were to be reckoned as the personal property of their owners, and liable to perform any service required of them, and disposable in any way their proprietors might choose.

4. That a master beating, or otherwise grossly ill-using his slave, without great and notorious cause of offence, was to be amenable to punishment; but when such cause had been given, a slave was liable to be tortured even with red-hot iron.

5. That a slave dying intestate, his owner was to become his heir-at-law, and inherit all his lands and effects.

An enactment so harsh and oppressive necessarily irritated the feelings of the native community. The odious distinction it made between the conquerors and the conquered struck them to the quick. The despotism of the British Government had for some time been regarded with the greatest hatred and dissatisfaction. But nothing—not the dishonest and inefficient administration of justice, not the gross corruption that prevailed in the highest functionaries of the Government, not even the total exclusion of the whole native population from every legitimate object of ambition, and every honourable species of employment—had spread such dissatisfaction, as this injudicious and disgraceful enactment. At first, from all quarters poured in entreaties, and appeals to good feeling. The *Morning Star*, the *Bengal Hurkaru*, and the *Agra Gazette* took up the cause of 'poor, oppressed India.' But entreaties, appeals to good feeling, and editoral declamations were of no avail. Then came the *Indian Patriot*,* denouncing the British Government, predicting its coming overthrow, philosophizing on the future, and calling on the slumbering genii of India to extirpate the foreigners. But the liberty of the Press was violated by the tyrannic Government, and the editor, proprietor, and printer were ordered to be imprisoned. This changed the state of affairs. The spirit of the populace

---

*This tale was written and originally published in 1845, or long before the *Hindu Patriot* was in existence. It is needless therefore to say that that paper is not referred to.

was kindled. On the north and on the south, on the east and on the west—everywhere, except in Pillibheet, the seat of empire—was raised the cry of revolt. All the provinces were in motion—thousands daily joined the standard of rebellion, and first and foremost ranked the insurgents of Orissá.

But the road was yet open for peace; though ripe for a revolt, the Indian army was, on proper terms, prepared to close the breach. But, elated with some heroic achievements on the frontiers of Cooch Behár, the Government refused to make the slightest concession; and this denial was made more poignant to the patriots by a very declamatory article in the *Government Advocate*, which denounced and ridiculed their exertions. The following is the article alluded to:—

'We think the glaring impolicy of taking up arms against the Government, adopted as it has been by the patriots of India, will be admitted by those who have their eyes open and their senses awake. Does it not strike the mind of every sensible man, that India, for centuries to come, will not be able to wrest the supremacy from the grasp of her conquerors? When we view the disparity in numbers between the black and white population, the result of this rebellion may be feared; but we shudder not for our brethren when we consider the comparative physical and moral courage of the parties pitted against each other. As well might you overpower the rushing leopard with a flock of sheep, as make Bheekoo Bárik, with a hundred *sowárs* at his back, confront the fiery visage of an English drunkard. Even if that were possible, would it not be the wiser plan for the patriots moderately to pursue that course which in time may place them on an equal footing with their conquerors, as regards the cultivation of intellect and the rules of civilized life, than to begin at the wrong end, and seek for freedom without having acquired the simplest lessons of government to secure that liberty? Do they presume, like the genii of Aláddin's lamp, to erect in one night a fair palace fit for the habitation of their deity? Are the Juggomohuns and Gocooldáses, the Opertis and Bindábun Sirdárs fit persons to be intrusted with the management of a vast empire? Though the liberty of India be a consummation devoutly to be wished for, yet must it be admitted that length of time is needful to erect that fabric. Says the common adage, "Rome was not built in a day." That under the British Government the Hindus are prospering, and will prosper in spite of their ingratitude, cannot be denied. Go a century or two backwards, take notes of other days, and compare India as it *was* with India as it *is*, and mark the result. But not yet are the Indians fit to be a free people. Perhaps, as time rolls on, the day may come when it will be unjust to refuse to, and perhaps impossible to withhold from the Indians the rights of liberty, and then England may possibly think it just and proper to relinquish her sovereignty over them—but not till then. The Hindus are like children. They want what they cannot understand, fret because with paternal care we refuse to indulge them, and cry because we are deaf to their entreaties. After all, what is there in the last enactment, which is held up as the immediate cause of sedition, to irritate their feelings? The harsher and more outrageous features of slavery have now no existence. Slavery, as now constituted, hardly approaches the "durance vile" of a common every-day labourer. To all intents and purposes the slave is as good as the *free* (?) labourer. But "why does the enactment exclude Europeans from slavery?" they ask. *Why*, dear patriots? Because ye are the conquered, we the conquerors. Are you answered?

'Ere taking leave of the subject, we will give a piece of advice to the insurgent chiefs, which we hope and wish for their own sakes they may not wholly despise. They should immediately disband their followers, come to the capital, and on their knees sue for pardon from the Government. We believe the Governor-General in Council may think it proper to excuse them and the people, on an adequate sum being raised for the erection of a palace, now in contemplation for the accommodation of his lordship's family. This measure, if they think proper to adopt it, should be taken before it is too late. We understand his lordship intends very soon to direct Sir George Proudfoot and the forces under his command to proceed, from the frontiers of Cooch Behár, where they are at present stationed, against the insurgent army now assembled at Beerbhoom.—29th Dec. 1917.'

This article highly incensed the patriot chiefs; and Bheekoo Bárik, the chief of the Kingáries of Orissá, was heard to say, 'My *sowárs* can confront the devil when he is mad, leave aside drunkards, English, Scotch, or Irish!' A convention of delegates from the insurgent forces of Bengal, Behár, and Orissá was held at Mulhárpore, on the 8th September, 1918; and it was there resolved that the British Government, having infringed the rules of good government, by introducing slavery into India, and by making various other innovations in the administration of the laws, which innovations were found upon experience to be highly injurious and despotic, it was necessary to adopt bold measures to prevent misrule; and the warriors all vowed to shed the last drops of their blood in the cause of freedom, if bloodshed should be necessary. It was also resolved that the insurgent army should be divided into two bodies—those of Bengal and Behár comprising one, and those of Orissá the other. Gokool Dás Treebaidy was chosen leader of the former, and Operti Sirdár of the latter.

It is not our purpose to give minute details of the wars that followed. An army of ten thousand Irish soldiers, under the command of Sir G. Proudfoot, was directed to proceed first against the forces of Bengal and Behár, and soon subjugating that body, marched in the winter of 1919 for Orissá. The invasion of Orissá was also attended with success at the outset; and success was attended with the most revolting cruelties. The fortress of Rádánuggur was taken at the point of the bayonet, no quarter was given, and the whole garrison was put to the sword; the sacred shrine of Sreekhettur was sacrilegiously pillaged; and Operti Sirdár was well-nigh overpowered on the plains of Parbutná, when the mounted troopers of Bheekoo Bárik rushed boldly to the teeth of the enemy, and scattered the whole army in complete rout.

This decisive victory of the Ooryáhs led to promises of concession on the part of the British Government; and, pleased with the prospects of peace, the patriot insurgents fell off. The British Council, in the meantime, perceiving that the immediate danger had passed away, forgot its promises, or deceitfully deferred fulfilling them. Matters were thus circumstanced, when a private wrong brought this uncertain state of affairs to a conclusion.

Lukhun Dás Khundáti, a hero of the good old times, who held a conspicuous station amongst his countrymen, and whose valour was known far beyond the confines of his nation, had a daughter named Nuleeny, a paragon of loveliness. This beauty was early betrothed to one Jugoo Dás Mytheepo, a young man of a very promising character, and, what is more consonant to the taste of women, cast in the best proportions of strength and manly beauty. Bred in the camp, and under the particular care and example of Lukhun Khundáti, he had imbibed all the manners that conspicuously marked the character of that hardy veteran. In every deed of desperation he had a heart to resolve, a head to contrive, and a hand to perform. This youth, while signalizing himself in a sally party by the most desperate feats of gallantry, had fallen prisoner into the hands of one Subadár Báhádoor Gopee Dás, an Ooryáh by birth, and a rejected admirer of Nuleeny, who had enlisted in the service of the enemies of his country on account of domestic differences. From him Jugoo Dás expected no fair treatment, and received none. His highest powers of endurance were put to the test; and his captor, making the public cause subservient to his private feelings, refused all proffers of a ransom and exchange of prisoners, and kept him chained and strictly guarded, no intercourse being allowed to be held with him.

It must not be imagined that, during this period, Lukhun Dás and his friends were unmindful of the valiant Jugoo. They tried every means for effecting his release; but Gopee Dás was deaf to their proffers and entreaties. Young hearts, however, are not easily put down; and the beautiful daughter of the Khundáti veteran was still planning and plotting for the escape of her lover, though hopelessness was depicted on the countenance of her father and the other elders of her country. With a spirit of chivalry which, in this age, is common amongst the women of no other country but Orissá, she left her father's house alone, disguised in the mean habiliments of a wandering *fakir*, to seek her beloved Jugoo among the hated Ferángees. What miseries and privations she suffered on the way, and how, when she did reach the place of her destination, she managed to ingratiate herself with her lover's captor, our deponent saith not; but that she succeeded in all this is placed beyond doubt by the fact that, in the course of a short time, having laid aside the dress of a *fakir*, and assumed that of a soldier, she was enlisted amongst his keepers. Not to make a romance of a simple matter of history we will at once inform our readers that, in this capacity, she managed to secure his liberty—not however so effectually as to prevent pursuit. Furious and foaming Gopee Dás gave chase, with half a dozen *sowárs* at his back; but Jugoo and his fair deliverer, being mounted on the fleetest horse ever transported from the happy shores of Arabia, were far out of harm's way.

It was not till they had reached the hills of Chotá Nágpore that their pursuers got sight of them. The *sowárs* pressed hard; and their cheers and the clatter of their horses' hoofs, sounded fearfully near in the ears of the fugitives. Every moment lessened the distance between them, till the space was reduced to an arm's length. The horse on which Jugoo and his betrothed were mounted, had cleared a greater space than any horse ever did, and could proceed no more. Now was the desperate moment. The young Mytheepo dismounted, and, like a lion at bay, turned back upon his pursuers, and single-handed opposed them all, resolved to sell his life as dearly as he could. Two of his assailants were levelled with the ground, and he was on the point of despatching a third, when a robust hávildár caught him by the neck and brought him down on his knees, and would have killed him, but that the beautiful Nuleeny, joining in the *mêlée*, plunged a dagger into the hávildár's heart. In the meantime, warding off the blows which were dealt at him from all sides, Jagoo kept rapidly retreating, until, gaining the brow of a steep declivity, he flung himself over to the opposite side, and was instantly lost to view. A desperate escape! And did he escape alone, leaving his liberator, his own Nuleeny, in the hands of his bitterest enemy? Even so. Not that he valued his life more than hers, but because he felt persuaded that she could meet no wrong from one who had long professed to be her lover. Gopee Dás was an Ooryáh, and Jugoo knew that his countrymen, of all nations in the world, were the most chivalrously devoted to the fair sex. How could Gopee, then, he reasoned internally, harm a woman? Unfortunately, he did not consider that an Ooryáh who had so far demeaned himself as to enter into the service of the Ferángees—*m'lechhas*, whose very touch is pollution—and to take up arms against his native country, could not possibly retain the noble nature of his race. Alas! sad was the fate of Nuleeny! But that fate was quickly avenged.

Lukhun Dás Khundáti was no sooner informed of his daughter's death, than he repaired to the Kingáries, or hill-tribes. He raked up the fire that was slumbering beneath the ashes, urged home the despotism of the British Government, and at the head of eighty thousand men, began his terrible march towards the English seat of empire, sweeping all petty detachments like dust before his path. The whole kingdom was once again in arms, and all with one accord shouted for battle. On the 15th of October, 1921, took place the memorable engagement of the Jumná, so named because fought on the banks of that sacred river. The English generals were totally defeated—their army cut down to a man. Jugoo Dás and Gopee Dás were found dead on the field of battle, locked fiercely in each other's arms! On the 13th January of the following year Orissá proclaimed her independence, and though the Government of Pillibheet refused to recognise it, their armies completely evacuated that province, after a few vain efforts to disturb its independence.

Years have passed over those events. The British Empire is sinking fast into that state of weakness and internal division which is the sure forerunner of the fall of kingdoms. Its former glory is now no more. But, with the usual inconsistency of human pride its tone was never more haughty, nor the exterior of its court ever more ostentatious.

'The shadow lengthens as the sun declines.'

We regret for its fallen grandeur; we regret to see an imperial bird, shorn of its wings and plumage of pride, coming down precipitately from its aëry height. The Council is still sitting, and is a scene of wrangling and confusion—a shadow of what it was, and a lively example of the insufficiency of regulation in a declining State. In the meantime, from this picture of fallen glory, and of the vicissitudes of human greatness, the eye is attracted by the morning splendour of a brilliant luminary. A splendid spectacle is presented to the eyes of wondering millions, of a nation emerging from the chaos of ignorance and slavery, and hastening to occupy its orbit on the grand system of civilization. The Republic of Orissá has become the predominant star in Hindustán.

A Journal of Forty-Eight Hours of the Year 1945
by Kylas Chunder Dutt. (A student at the Hindoo College.)

[from *The Calcutta Literary Gazette, or, Journal of Belles Lettres, Science, and the Arts*, Vol. III, new series, no. 75 (6th June 1835)]

And shall we, shall men, after five and twenty years of ignominious servitude, shall we, through a fear of dying, defer one single instant to assert our liberty? No, Romans; now is the time; the favorable moment we have so long waited for is come.

Junius Brutus[55]

The people of India and particularly those of the metropolis had been subject for the last fifty years to every species of subaltern oppression. The dagger and the bowl were dealt out with a merciless hand, and neither age, sex, nor condition could repress the rage of the British barbarians. These events, together with the recollection of the grievances suffered by their ancestors, roused the dormant spirit of the generally considered timid Indian. Finding that every day the offences instead of being extenuated were aggravated, that no redress could be obtained by appeals to either Lords or Commons, he formed the bold but desperate resolution of hurling Lord Fell Butcher, viceroy of India, from his seat and establishing a government composed of the most patriotic men in the kingdom. It is neither a matter of surprise nor for indignation, that the born subjects of 'the lord's anointed' of merry England should take up arms against their sovereign, when we consider the deep and dreadful provocations which the Indians received. It was the only method calculated to repress the brutal atrocities of the merciless conquerors. Men accustomed to scenes of dangerous intrigue and infamous cruelty soon become callous to the generous feelings of human nature. With the rapidity of lightning the spirit of Rebellion spread through this once pacific people. It is easy for the historian and the bard to depict in the most lively colours the excesses committed by revolutionary parties, but he only can truly judge of their situation who has been a fellow sufferer with those whose families, friends and companions have been butchered in cold blood—who has seen villages and towns laid waste by fire for illumination—who has beheld thousands of human beings compelled to desert their home and country and seek refuge in dens of the earth, in clefts of rocks or in the hollows of trees.

In this conspiracy were engaged many of the most distinguished men in Calcutta—Bábús, Rájás and Nabábs increased its consequence. It was conducted for some time with the greatest imaginable secrecy, and the contagion of Rebellion would probably have infested every city in the kingdom, had it only had time to perfect its machinations.

It was a beautiful evening; the hues of the setting sun, the whisper of breezes and the singing of birds made the whole scene delightful. Instead of lounging about the streets, as is generally the case, the rich and poor all huddled in the same direction. At about six a vast number of men assembled on the North Eastern suburbs of the 'City of Palaces.'[56] On the left of this spacious plain gurgles a rill, on the right it is fenced by avenues of bamboos. The front view is bounded by a beautiful Pagoda, the work of some Moslem hand, whose spiral tops reflected in a thousand fantastic colours the bright rays of the sinking sun. Within this inclosure, all was lovely—the tumultuous dashing of the waters, the hollow murmurs of the winds, and the confused melody of singing birds and human voices, made it inexpressibly enchanting. The people all sat down on the turf and the proceedings of the meeting commenced. From one extremity rose a venerable figure not above fifty or sixty. The contracted brow and the deep furrows on his cheeks marked the predominance of passion and of corroding care over age. 'Gentlemen,' said he, 'I have the pleasure once more of witnessing my fellow countrymen, assembled to assert their native rights and vindicate their wrongs. But before we enter upon this day's topic, allow me to ask whether the proposition of each man wearing a carabine and a sword, carried at our last meeting, has been universally complied with?' A loud and lengthened peal of applause proved that it was. Bhoobun Mohun, a youth of twenty-five splendidly attired in kincaub and gold, rose at the instant his venerable predecessor extended himself on the turf. He gracefully flung a richly embroidered scarf over his left shoulder and addressed the meeting with all the learning and eloquence which the Anglo-Indian College could furnish. He expatiated with a deep manly tone on the hardships and dangers to which the natives of Indostan had been subject since their subjugation by the Britons; and concluded by saying, 'My friends and countrymen, I speak not to you with a wish to display my powers of rhetoric (of which I possess but little), I am not speaking from a heated imagination or blind enthusiasm, I speak only the plain and simple dictates of my heart, which I firmly believe meet with a response in all your bosoms. Consider for a moment the cruelties which from generation to generation you have suffered. What improvements in our condition could be expected from the enormities of Clive, the despotism of Wellesley, the wanton cruelty of Warren Hastings[57] and the inordinate rapacity of our present odious Government? While the other nations of the earth are rising high in the scale of civilization, the people of Indostan are daily sinking to the level of beasts. Consider for a moment, my friends and countrymen! of what you have been forcibly bereft by these rough islanders. If you are still willing to submit to the wicked impositions of the British nation, if you are still willing to bear patiently all the refined cruelties of our present ruler Lord Fell Butcher, if your hearts sicken not at the idea of degradation, if your feelings revolt not at the thought of shackles and dungeons, I shall set you down for the most abject and degraded of human beings. But banish that thought. Let us unanimously engage to emancipate the natives from the thraldom of oppression. Let us all unite in a body, and it shall be the most glorious scene that India has beheld, when we effect the overthrow by one powerful and deadly blow of this system of injustice and rapacity.'

'Friends! countrymen and chieftains! let us no more be called the weak, the deluded portion of mankind, let us no more be branded with cowardice and degeneration, let us unfurl the banner of Freedom and plant it where Britannia* now proudly stands. If the consideration of rising in the estimation of the world move you not, Oh! I beseech you to look for the safety of the dear companions of your souls, the little ones, the darling of your eyes, and above all attend to the wants of our much neglected mother, the land that gave us birth.'

There was a murmur of approbation and a burst of applause as soon as the young man concluded his harangue and sat amongst a group of acquaintances. In the mean time many of the audience at once exclaimed 'Red coats! Red coats!' On looking forward it was perceived that about 16 troopers and 150 dismounted dragoons were approaching the spot where they were assembled. They all jumped up and Bhoobun Mohun whistled shrilly, which was answered from some distance by the report of a gun. The little body of soldiery immediately appeared on the skirts of the plain. Two officers dressed in scarlet and gold led or rather hauled a stout looking civilian between them. The man in black, evidently terrified on seeing so vast a concourse before him, could neither walk nor speak. Being reminded by the officers to do his duty, he with no little hesitation and change of countenance read the proclamation for dispersion. The bold patriotic youth retorted nearly in the following words. 'Worthy Magistrate, I am sorry we are not able to

*The top of the Government House.

comply with your proposition; we defy you to do your worst. You see before you men who will neither be terrified by the neighing of a steed, the waving of a sword nor the flashing of a gun. We are determined to assert our liberties, when every other resource has failed, by the strength of our arms. Go tell them that sent thee that we have resolved to hurl Fell Butcher from his seat, we have renounced the allegiance of the feeble and false Harry of England, and that we mean to abide by our own laws and parliaments!' Confounded at this bold declaration, the good magistrate staggered back a few paces and was supported by a serjeant from sinking to the ground. The officers looked at each other, whispered a few words and the trumpets sounded a charge with bayonets. The youthful hero blew a shrill blast, and about two hundred turbaned figures with guns in their hands, and fifty horsemen with scimitars and lances, appeared from the side which was covered by bamboos. The unarmed retired to the borders of the plain, while a general engagement took place between the patriots and the royalists, both charged with levelled bayonets alternately retiring and advancing. The clashing of swords, the discharge of guns, the shrieks of the wounded and the groans of the dying made a fearful noise. During this bloody transaction our hero was not a silent spectator of the scene. He ordered his attendant to bring his proud war horse, and having adjusted his clothes with military nicety, he buckled his pistols round his waist, waved his sword and mounted his charger. Receiving the benediction of the venerable priest who stood trembling a few paces distant, and whispering a prayer to Heaven to strengthen his arm, he darted himself into the midst of the fray. Lieutenant Martin, mad with rage, confronted him and aimed a furious blow at him which he eluded with great dexterity. Escaping the blow, he in his turn gave a smart rap on the head of his antagonist, which made him reel in his saddle for a minute or two. 'Curse on the barbarian,' said he, and renewed the combat with redoubled ardour. The contest was long and furious, the coolness and agile movements of the Hindoo being a counterpoise to the great strength of the Briton. They exchanged many smart cuts, their rich and splendid dresses were hacked and hewn in a thousand places, and the nodding plume of the one and the flowing scarf of the other were mangled and torn to atoms in the fray. At length the Briton foaming with ire and exhausted with loss of blood, muttering the direst of oaths of vengeance, recoiled from his saddle and fell headlong on the ground. Victory declared in favor of the patriots. About twenty-five royalists lay dead on the plain and as many wounded; while of the patriots six had expired and thirteen were severely bruised. The remaining officers of the royalists, consulting for a minute or two together, ordered the trumpets to sound a retreat. Forming themselves into three bodies they retired one by one, keeping their front towards the enemy, who continued a brisk fire. The night having advanced pretty far the patriots betook themselves to their houses to dream of their glorious exploits and to rise in the morning to consult new plans for the furtherance of their object.

We must now conduct the reader to the magnificent apartments of the Government House, the residence of the noble and humane Lord Fell Butcher. The door of the bed chamber being slowly opened by the surdar bearer a damsel apparently of 14 with luxuriant tresses and deep black eyes, having about her a short robe of fine white linen with long white sleeves, was discovered arranging her dress. The skirts of her robe hung down as far as the knee, displaying the calf of her leg and the delicate symmetry of her ancles and feet. Her shoes were of the most curious workmanship and a checquered silk handkerchief carelessly thrown about her neck, vied in splendour with the hues of the rainbow. An image of some Deity set with diamonds and pearls was suspended round her neck to protect her from evil. As soon as she placed her light foot upon the threshold, the Viceroy waked and jumped out of his bed and asked the bearer whether 'Beeby sahib' was stirring. Being answered in the negative, he conducted the damsel along the marble pavements, and placing her in the palanquin, took a hearty farewell. The morning ablutions being over, he entered the Council Hall with the morning gazette in his hand. It was splendidly furnished—chandeliers, mirrors, pictures, arras and carpets made a gorgeous display. In the middle was placed a small table with heaps of folded letters, rolled up parchments and writing materials. After perusing the gazette for a minute or two he laid it aside and exclaimed who waits? A young officer, his hat under his arm and his sword dangling by his side, appeared, made a low respectful bow and approached his lordship. 'Ho! What is d'ye call him, here?' 'Yes, my lord, ensign Valancourt stays without.' 'Bid him come hither.' The officer retired and in a minute or two the ensign entered the hall. His face was patched in five or six different places and his left hand was tied in a sling. 'Well sir, I hope the business of yesterday has been gloriously terminated?' The officer hung down his head and the blood gushed into his features. 'Ah! ha! is that the case? Did the royalists retreat before a parcel of Bengalees? We must take severer measures now I should think. Well how many wounded and killed?' 'Fifty, my lord.' 'Zounds! that's terrible. How did the riotous mob contrive to send so many to Pluto's gloomy region?' 'There was a body of two or three hundred men in ambush armed at all points, who seeing us attack the rebellious mob with our bayonets, rushed into the conflict and—' 'Made you turn your heels?' The ensign again blushed and hung down his head. 'I shall see. You may go; but remain within hearing.' Making a profound bow, the young man retired. After taking two or three turns about the room in deep meditation, his Lordship resumed his chair and penned the following letter.

To COL. JOHN BLOOD-THIRSTY.

The town and fort Major of the Fort William in Bengal.

My Dear Col. —It appears from the information of many confidential persons that great dissatisfaction towards Government is prevalent amongst the native population. I authorize you therefore to take such measures as will be requisite for the safety of the Fort in case of a surprise or sudden attack. The publicity attending the transmission of letters through Secretaries and Boards has obliged me to have recourse to this method.

I am, my dear Col.

Your's sincerely,

Govt. House, April, 1945.   BUTCHER

Dispatching this letter, he took a turn or two and wrote the following paragraph, which he sent to the press.

THE CALCUTTA COURIER EXTRAORDINARY,

April 1945.

We understand from a military person, that last evening a party consisting of two troopers and sixteen foot soldiers were sent by Government to quell the disturbances of two thousand men in the neighbourhood of Calcutta. The Magistrate tried his utmost efforts to persuade the people to return to their houses, but all in vain: they persisted in keeping their ground. The military, according to the orders of the Lieut. in command, made a mock fire, which so terrified the vast multitude that they fled in every direction. Some persons were crushed to death in the dense crowd and some were drowned in attempting to cross the stream. Be that as it may, the affair of yesterday has been, without the effusion of blood, a terrible example to the disturbers of the peace. ———

When Boohun Mohun returned home from the dreadful rencontre, various thoughts crossed his mind. Sleep fled from his troubled pillow, and he lay motionless on his bed in deep reverie, and at last starting up he exclaimed, 'I must chase these idle fears and dire forebodings.' He sent for some of the principal conspirators, who arrived soon after; and consulted with them on the requisite manœuvres and the probable result of their intended attack on the Fort. 'If we do not,' said he, 'take advantage of this favorable moment, will not search warrants be issued to-morrow for the bodies of Bhoobun Mohun, Parbutty Churn and Gunganarain, or a price set on their rebellious heads. Information will be communicated to night to all the stations near Calcutta, and ere tomorrow noon thousands of horse all in complete array, and hundreds of twenty-four pounders, glancing against the sun, will occupy the Esplanade and even the streets of Calcutta. But then where is the remedy? The expected succours have not yet arrived, and the flower of our countrymen have been too much fatigued by the bloody and obstinate engagement of this evening to hazard the surprise of the fort or the blowing up of the government house to night.' The consultation proceeded till 2 A.M. when convinced of their own importance and flushed with their trifling victory, they determined on attacking the fort the next day at nightfall. The parties separated with the full expectation that ere day-break the promised supplies of men and money would reach them and that the next day's sun would be as propitious as the preceding day's.

The dawn of morning roused Bhoobun Mohun, and its light was scarcely abroad in the azure heavens, when a gentle tap at the door of his dwelling announced some friendly visitor. It was slowly opened, and a man delivered a scroll into the hands of our hero. He read it attentively more than once, and then as if unconscious of the presence of any one, said, 'why say "dear Bhoohun and your's affectionately" when you do not mean it? Why not tell me at once that you were afraid of your family, your head, and above all your purse. Silly fool, that I was, to have trusted so much in your "utmost efforts to further our cause, your not caring to be made a beggar or what is worse your indifference as to the possibility of your loosing your head." Ah! ha! I see through all. Now that the thing becomes more and more dangerous you wish to'—Perceiving that the servant who brought the letter was listening patiently to all his unconscious remarks, he looked at him full in the face, with a keenly scrutinizing eye and then imperatively bade him depart. Returning to his closet, he re-perused the letter with a deep emotion and then muttered to himself. 'I must do, I see, without these cowardly hinds. The work must not be delayed any longer.' During the day he employed himself in writing to all his faithful comrades, informing them of the propriety of the speedy termination of this affair. Night came on, and the assembled force of the insurgents seemed to be considerable; the whole of the Chitpore road and part of the Esplanade was densely occupied. Nothing was to be seen but turbaned heads, pikes, muskets and halberts—reflecting in glittering colors the pale beams of the moon.

While the artillery-men on the ramparts were preparing some guns to give the insurgents an idea of the warm reception which they were to receive in a closer engagement, a rebel horseman displayed a large white pennon. Gunganarain, for such was the equestrian's name, a robust looking youth, spurred his horse, which dance and galloped to the sound of martial music and was in a short time within pistol shot from the fort. On seeing him approach thus far, the draw-bridge was lowered and some men dressed like officers, advancing to receive his message, fairly surrounded him. Without being in the least daunted, the youth told them in a loud, strong voice, that he had been commissioned by the only supreme power in this country, the leaders of the national convention, to summon them in the name of the convention, to surrender the castle, to lay down their arms and dismiss the native troops in their employ upon fair conditions of quarter and licence to depart with their families and property. 'In case of a refusal,' he continued, 'mark the consequence! Fire and sword shall soon destroy you.' No sooner was this pronounced, than as if by one impulse, three or four of the officers laid strong hold of his arm, while two caught hold of the bridle and dragged him violently into the fort. Wondering at this circumstance, the insurgent army waited in anxious suspense for the conclusion of such extraordinary behaviour. After a few minutes, as if every thing was ready for the purpose, the poor man was seen swinging, like a pendulum, on a gibbet upon one of the ramparts, shorn of his splendid robes and having a paper crown on his head, in derision of the assumed title of his rebellious party. This became the signal for a general onset, and several hundred cavaliers putting their horses into motion, rode furiously up, followed by a strong and disciplined band of foot soldiers, to avenge the cruel death of their young officer. The whole army would have fallen into confusion, but for the timely aid of its experienced officers, who flew from rank to rank, entreating, commanding and menacing the men to keep their ground. As they discharged their fire-arms against the defenders upon the battlements, they were hailed by a shower of cannon balls, which emptied at least two score of saddles. Continuing with determined courage to ascend the walls, and being vigorously supported by a strong body of men-at-arms, which was brought up with admirable skill, they sustained with firmness another heavy but much more destructive fire. Possessing no means to protect themselves from this galling fire or of answering it even with their guns, the royalists being under cover of their barricades and other defences, the insurgents were in the most dreadful situation. To their great alarm, also they beheld a body of horsemen, the body guards of the viceroy stationed at Ballygunge, amounting to about six hundred men approaching to relieve the garrison. The horsemen charged furiously and another terrible fire was opened from the government house, in which were placed a body of infantry. In the mean time Bhoobun Mohun, perceiving to his great mortification the inevitable consequence of this rash engagement, fought with desperation. Most of his followers were killed and he himself would have met with the same fate but for the successful exertions of a cool and resolute company of soldiers, who poured a heavy fire of carabines wherever they advanced. Extricating himself from his present difficulty, he began to rally his forces, that were scattered in every direction. An officer hastily rode up to him and met him face to face. Without any other introduction than that of *the friend of Lieutenant Martin*, he attacked Bhoobun Mohun with the greatest fury, but light of foot and quick of eye, the latter leaped aside and eluded a blow which would have proved fatal had it taken effect. Exchanging many smart cuts and desperate blows, they rushed towards each other and grasping one another's clothes they furiously grappled together like two desperate gladiators. The contest continued for several minutes, during which time their deadly clasp was not loosened; and at last, as if actuated by a demon, they both let go their hold, and foaming with ire, flourished their weapons and made a terrible pass. The sword of the officer grazed the ribs of Bhoobun Mohun, while that of our redoubted hero passed right through his opponent's heart. The gigantic Englishman fell prostrate on the ground with a groan that marked his instant dissolution. Taking a minute's rest, after so warm a contest, Bhoobun Mohun began to rally round him his scattered troops and signified his intention of consulting with his officers, some of whom formed a circle round him. While he was in this situation, the draw-bridges were unexpectedly lowered, the garrison sallied out, and a severe action commenced in which the patriot and his men displayed the most determined valour. The scene became still more horrible. On one side the patriots were charged by bayonets, on another they were attacked by the bodyguard, while from a third, the artillery made a lamentable havoc. The youthful hero toiled in the front excessively, encouraging, by his resolute, brave and cool behaviour, the rest of his countrymen who harassed on all sides were unable to keep the field any longer; the better part of the troops rushed desperately into the conflict, unawed either by the number or the success of the enemy, while the less brave or more wearied hastened to hide themselves in streets and houses from the excesses of an enraged and victorious soldiery. Every moment reinforcements poured out from the fort and the strife continued, even then, with great fury between thousands on one side and a handful of men on the other. Sure of the dreadful result, the patriots were still reluctant to quit the field. Fifty men out of many thousands alone remained on the spot to contend for the liberties of their country. Had there been light sufficient to distinguish friend from foe, they too would inevitably have been crushed to death, but the disappearance of the moon and the smoke of the fire arms tended greatly to their safety. While they were in this precarious situation, the dawn of morning was visible, which increasing made known to the English, the smallness of the enemy's troops. There was a furious charge from every direction and the handful of men, after maintaining the contest, so long undecided, was nearly annihilated—twenty-five were instantly slain, fifteen severely wounded and ten taken prisoners. The trampling of horses, the shrieks of the wounded and the groans of the dying made the scene extremely fearful. It was found on the closer examination that the leader of the patriotic party was not amongst those who made the grass their bed, but was a prisoner in the fort, along with nine other men. There was a shrill cry of savage joy and wild exultation as this was signified to the whole body of the soldiery. The military formed themselves into lines and entered the fort, the musicians playing the triumphant airs of victory. Spurring the horses and making them leap twelve feet at a bound, the officers—their swords dyed in blood and their uniforms besmeared with dirt—joined the dreadful shouts of revelry.—

Hope for a season bade the world farewell
And freedom shrieked as *India's patriot* fell.

There was a general silence when the Cathedral bell tolled six. People from the different quarters of the city began to assemble on the esplanade at the front of the government house. The countenances of the European spectators exhibited a brutal triumph while those of the natives betrayed despair. A quarter after six, it was announced that the prisoner's car was approaching its destination. Every eye was directed to the place whence the carriage issued. A band of musicians playing the dead march formed the van, their measured steps and stately appearance tending to increase the general melancholy. Behind them came a little square consisting of a hundred men with halberts, followed by the expected car which was surrounded by two circles of dismounted dragoons. Their nodding plumage, glittering bayonets and scarlet coats made a terrific display. The rear was closed by one regiment of foot, the 13th I believe, and about two hundred well built troopers. With solemn steps and slow they entered the government house by the large archway opposite Esplanade row. The cavalcade made a halt and arranged themselves according to directions. The regiment of foot was stationed in two opposite rows east to west, and the battalion of horse stood parallel to the house; that the view might not be obstructed; nothing else was placed between it and a *scaffold*, save one or two solitary sentinels, who viewed the whole scene with intense anxiety. As the gentlemen, the friends of *our* noble lord arrived, their steeds were taken to the stables, where the attendants employed themselves in freeing the animals of their gorgeous trappings and decorations; which were as various as the taste, caprice or the means of the owners. The guests were ushered into the great hall where was a table groaning under the weight of Asiatic luxuries. As the upper end of the table sat the humane viceroy, who welcomed his friends and invited them with politeness to partake of his *simple* cheer. Before their hungry appetites the board was soon cleared and the most merciful ruler of India with all his friends and retinue arranged themselves on benches opposite the windows, to feast their eyes with the approaching glorious sight. A signal being made by the firing of a gun to prepare the prisoner, the door of the huge vehicle was slowly opened by a serjeant, with three files of soldiers standing by him. He was brought out and exposed to the public gaze. The same bold spirit which had distinguished him in the heat of contest, still shone in his features. His hair was dishevelled, his clothes out of order and his hands and legs closely fettered—every thing marked his sad destiny save that sternness of demeanour, which struck terror into the minds of those who beheld him. A smith who stood at a respectful distance was now beckoned to do his duty. The 'cold bonds' were struck off and he was conducted to the scaffold. A tall, well-built man stood at one extremity of it with a heavy axe in his hand. With a determined step the prisoner strode upon the stage and eyed the whole scene with perfect self-possession. He knelt down for a moment, placed his hands over his eyes, uttered a few indistinct words towards Heaven—a momentary hectic flushed his countenance and the he rose with his usual activity. Intending to address the people, he walked manfully up to the front of the stage, and the following words burst forth from his lips. 'My friends and countrymen! I have the consolation to die in my native land, and tho' Heaven has doomed that I should expire on the scaffold, yet are my last moments cheered by the presence of my friends. I have shed my last blood in defence of my country and though the feeble spark within me is about to leave its frail frame, I hope you will continue to persevere in the course you have so gloriously commenced.'

While he was going on in this strain, the viceroy struck with awe at the energy of the young patriot, dispatched an officer to conclude the scene immediately. His hands were powerfully arrested, his head forcibly thrust between two wooden pillars and severed from his body at a single blow.[58]

Notes

Reminiscences of a Keráni's Life

1. *The admirable Crichton.* James Crichton, a widely travelled sixteenth-century Scottish poet and adventurer, is the subject of a story in Thomas Urquhart's *Ekskubalauron* ('The Jewel') of 1651. Shoshee would probably have been more familiar with a later version of Crichton's life, William Harrison Ainsworth's popular historical novel *Crichton,* published in 1837.
2. *Bacon, Addison and Johnson.* Philosophers and writers popular with students of the Hindu College. Francis Bacon (1561-1626), philosopher and author of the *Novum Organum* and the utopian *New Atlantis.* Joseph Addison (1672-1719), poet and playwright. Samuel Johnson (1709-84), essayist, critic and lexicographer.
3. *A pass for his salt.* A heavy tax was imposed on salt by the East India Company on all Britain's Indian subjects after Clive's victory at the battle of Plassey in 1757. Gandhi made it the focus of one of his civil disobedience campaigns in 1931, when he marched to Dandi beach to make salt.
4. *Afghan War.* The First Anglo-Afghan War took place in 1838 and lasted four years. After deposing the Afghan ruler, Dost Mohammed, and installing Shah Soojah in his place, the British faced resistance from disaffected Afghan tribes who flocked to support Dost Mohammed's son. British involvement ended with the disastrous evacuation of the British garrison to Jalalabad during which Ghilzai warriors killed most of the evacuees.
5. *Shah Soojah.* The puppet-leader installed in Kabul by the British during the First Afghan War.
6. *Spence's.* The first large hotel to open in Calcutta, *circa* 1830.
7. *The mysteries of Calcutta.* Shoshee is referring obliquely to G. W. M. Reynolds' melodramatic novel series *The Mysteries of London* (1844-48) which was very popular in India. For a discussion of Reynolds' Indian readership, see Priya Joshi, *In Another Country: Colonialism, Culture, and the English Novel in India* (New York: Columbia University Press, 2002).
8. *Dr Johnson's …letter to Lord Chesterfield.* A famous letter, written in 1755, in which Johnson eloquently snubs Lord Chesterfield. Johnson had sought Lord Chesterfield's patronage early in his career, but was rebuffed, and received no help or notice from him until after his dictionary had been completed and he no longer needed a patron.
9. *B boo.* i.e. Báboo: typographical error.
10. *Springes to catch woodcocks. Hamlet,* I. 3. 115.
11. *Soonderbuns.* The Sundarbans, a forested river-delta area south of Calcutta.

12. *Joe Miller.* A comedian whose name was used posthumously to entitle the book *Joe Miller's Jests*, first published in 1739 and reissued throughout the eighteenth and nineteenth centuries; Joe Miller thereby became synonymous with old jokes.

13. *Maecenas.* Born between 74 and 64 BC, a Roman statesman and wealthy patron of Horace, Virgil and and Propertius, Maecenas' name is now associated with munificent literary patronage.

14. *Sir Henry Hardinge.* 1785-1856. British Field Marshal and Governor General of India between 1844 and 1848.

15. *Laplace and Newton.* Pierre-Simon Laplace (1749-1827) was a French mathematician who pioneered astronomical mechanics and probability mathematics. Isaac Newton (1642-1727) was a mathematician and physicist who revolutionized the study of optics, calculus, and gravitation.

16. *She has to feed so many drones.* The realization that Britain's profits from revenues and trade in India far exceeded colonial investment and development in the country would later form an important part of nationalist thinking. It was the basis of Dadabhai Naoroji's 'drain theory' and informed Romesh Chunder Dutt's economic studies of famine of India.

17. *Peel's brigade.* Also called the Naval Brigade, a colonial relief force set up in August 1857 by the former British Prime Minister's son, Captain William Peel, using men and cannons from warships HMS *Shannon* and HMS *Pearl.*

18. *Ugolino.* Ugolino della Gherardesca. A thirteenth-century Italian Guelf leader and master of Pisa who was known for his treachery. He was betrayed, imprisoned in a tower, and starved to death. He narrates his story in Dante's *Inferno,* xxxiii.

19. *Áhriman and Áhoormazd.* Oppositional religious figures from the Avesta, the principle sacred text of Zoroastrianism and basis of the Parsi faith. *Áhoormazd* is a transcription of *Ahura Mazda*, the creator-deity of Zoroatsrianism, and *Áhriman* is one of the two twin spirits he produced, who subsequently became evil and turned against him.

Shunkur: A tale of the Indian Mutiny of 1857

20. *Some foreign power.* Shoshee hints here that the Mutiny was instigated (in part) by secret agents working for the Russians. Throughout the mid- to late nineteenth century the British were wary of Russian imperial ambitions, especially in India's North West Frontier.

21. *Conversion of the natives of India.* A number of rumours that the British were planning a mass conversion of South Asians and were adulterating foodstuffs in defiance of Hindu and Muslim holy law circulated before the Mutiny.

22. *Our past glory.* The revival of historical accounts of Rajput and Maratha valour were integral to the growth of regional nationalism in Bengal in the late nineteenth century. Nostalgia for a lost Vedic 'Golden Age' also formed the basis of discourses of Aryan primordial identity.

The Street-Music of Calcutta

23. *Kooar-ghotee-tolláh.* 'Lost pitchers or buckets retrieved' from a well. Subsequent translations of street-cries in these notes are not literal. Where necessary a more exact, supplementary translation appears in brackets.

24. *The Moorish lady.* A reference to 'Zara's Earrings', a medieval Spanish ballad of Moorish origins. In the ballad Zara, daughter of Albuharez, laments the loss of a pair of earrings given to her by her lover Muca. See Charles F. Horne, ed., *The Sacred Books and Early Literature of the East, Vol. VI: Medieval Arabia.* (New York: Parke, Austin and Lipscomb, 1917), pp. 245-55.

25. *Old Bazaine's escape.* Achille François Bazaine (1811-1888) was a French officer who served in the Franco-Prussian war and became a supreme commander under Napoleon III. He was convicted of treason in 1873 and imprisoned in Fort St Marguerite, but managed to escape and spent the rest of his life in exile in Italy and Spain.

26. *Mákhum chorá.* Legendary thief—in this case Krishna.

27. *Jye Rádhay! Bhikayápye bábá?* 'Victory to Radha! Alms, sir?'

28. *Sissee, bottole bikree!* 'Phials, bottles to sell?'

29. *Pooráná kágoch!* 'Any old paper?'

30. *Pooráná lohá bikree!* 'Any old iron to sell?'

31. *Pooráná cháttá bikree!* 'Any old umbrellas to sell?'

32. *Pooráná nakra káni bikree!* 'Any old drums, trumpets [or musical instruments]?'

33. *Kátáo seel-cháktee jántá!* 'Flat mortars and grinding stones [re-]cut!'

34. *Bhálo bhálo ...* 'Roll up, roll up, see the new snake and monkey show' [literally, 'good good new new snake and monkey entertainment'].

35. *Chye moong-ke dál?* 'Lentils for sale!'

36. *Hánsayr deem chye ...* 'Duck eggs, buy my duck eggs!'

37. *Belátee ámrá chye ...* 'British plums for sale; nuts and almonds' [the adjective *Belátee* refers here to the good quality of the fruit, not its origin].

38. *Áloo chye; Piáz chye?* 'Any potatoes? Any rice?'

39. *Menu and Vyasa.* Legendary Hindu sages. The great Vedic treatise on law, the *Manusmriti*, is attributed to Manu, and was compiled between 200 BC and AD 200. The scribe Vyasa, also called *Krsna Dvaipayana* or *Vedavyasa*, is thought to have lived around 1500 BC, and is said to be the compiler of the epic poem the *Mahaharata.*

40. *Chye málsee dohi ...* 'Have a pot of yoghurt!'

41. *Choree libee go!* 'Buy some bangles!'

42. *Ghotee bátee sárábay ...* 'Pitchers, cups, lampstands repaired!'

43. *Ripoor kormo!* 'Any darning?'

44. *Salie Jooteá; Jootá broosh!* 'Shoes cobbled; shoe brushes!'

45. *Do golie sootá ek pysá!* 'Two rolls of cotton for one paisa!'

46. *Dhámá bándábay go!* 'Baskets woven!'

47. *Báxo sártay áchay?* 'Any boxes to repair?'

48. *Járuck laboo ...* 'Pickled lemon, fruit conserves, digestive pills, mango pickle, sweets, mango chutney.'

49. *Mondá Metoy!* 'Boiled sweets!'

50. *Rootee, biskoot ...* 'Bread, biscuits.'

51. *Golápee aooree ...* 'Beans for sale.'

52. *Nakole dáná.* 'Toffees.'

53. *Chanachoor, Boruph.* See glossary.

54. *Yápeed Mooshkilláshán Karaygá.* 'All problems will be solved.' Shoshee's observation that Hindu housewives regularly gave alms to petition a Muslim saint suggests that popular forms of devotional Hindu and Muslim faith were characterized by a degree of syncretism in contemporary Calcutta.

A Journal of Forty-Eight Hours

55. *Junius Brutus.* A character in *Coriolanus*, although the epigraph is not a quotation from Shakespeare's play. Shoshee may be referring to a play of the same name by William Duncombe.

56. *City of palaces.* Calcutta.

57. *Clive, Wellesley, Warren Hastings.* Important figures in the history of early British colonial rule in India. Robert Clive (1725-1774) played a pivotal role in consolidating the East India Company's rule in Bengal after the battle of Plassey in 1757. Clive was suspected of corruption but was acquitted of the charge on his return to Britain in 1767. Richard Wellesley (1760-1842) was made governor-general of India in 1797, and oversaw the expansion of British colonial rule in South India and the Deccan. Warren Hastings (1732-1818), the first governor-general of India, was, like Clive, prosecuted for extortion in a very public trial in London in 1788, but was acquitted in 1795.

58. *His head ... severed from his body at a single blow.* Although the public execution of rebels would become commonplace during and after the Mutiny (a new, horrifying method being to tie the prisoner in front of field-cannons), decapitation was not the usual form of execution in India in the 1830s. In fact this scene, with its description of 'two wooden pillars', owes more to literary descriptions of the use of the guillotine during the French revolution.

Glossary

ámláh	Bureaucrat.
anna	Small coin, one sixteenth of a rupee.
ássá	Tribal group.
áttá	Flour.
áttur	Extract of rose water. Perfumed essential oil.
Báboo / Bábú	Indian educated in English; a clerk able to write in English.
Báhádoor	Champion or hero. Honorific title given to deputy magistrates in the East India Company.
bazaár	Marketplace.
Begum	Senior matron in a middle-class Muslim household.
bikreewállá	Bottle-dealer.
Bráhman	Brahmin: the highest, priest-caste in Hinduism.
brandy-páwny	Brandy and water.
budmásh	Rogue, a troublemaker.
burophwállá	Ice-seller.
burrá báboo	Senior (bilingual) clerk.
Burrá Huzoor	Honorific title for a boss or manager.
Burrá Sáheb	Senior European master / boss.
bursátee cháttás	Umbrella [literally, 'rain parasol' from Hindi *barsat*].
bustee	Makeshift shelter.
buxis	Alms, a tip [from Persian *baksheesh*].
chabáná	Pastry, a type of snack.
chádur	Wrap or shawl.
challán	Bank draft.
Chamar	Member of an 'untouchable' sweeper caste.
chánáchoor	Fried snack made from a mixture of chickpeas, nuts and spices.
chánáchoor Gurmá-Gurrum	The above, freshly prepared.

chapprássie	Cashier.
cháttá	Parasol.
chillum	Straight clay pipe, often fitted to a Hookah. Used for smoking tobacco or cannabis.
chirág	Lamp.
chogá	Long-sleeved garment like a dressing gown.
chooree	Thin glass bangle.
Chotá Sáheb	'Little Master', a more junior European administrator [from Urdu *Sahib*: friend, lord]
chundan	1) Mixed lime-flavoured salt [from Urdu *Chooran*]. 2) Sandalwood [from Bangla *Chondon*].
chuppáties	Dry wheatflour pancake.
churus	Cannabis resin, a narcotic.
cooly	Unskilled labourer.
cowrie	Seashell used as small-denomination coinage.
dákhillá	Banker's receipt.
dál	Cooked lentils.
Dasahárá	Hindu winter festival.
dewán	Minister in charge of the finances of an Indian state.
doolies	Covered litter. Cheaper and lighter than a palanquin.
duftry	Secretarial under-clerk, employed to rule lines, mend pens, and make envelopes.
durwán	Doorkeeper, gate-porter [from Persian *darwān*].
fakir	Hindu sadhu or holy-man.
Ferángee	European; a derogatory term (a corruption of 'Franks').
flash house	Brothel.
gállee	To swear.
ganjá	Dried cannabis leaves, smoked as a narcotic.
ghárry	Horse-drawn carriage.
ghee	Clarified butter.
gold-mohurs	Gold coin introduced by the Mughals, and used by the East India Company. Worth 16 rupees in 1818.
gooroo	Hindu spiritual teacher [from Hindi *Guru*].
gram	Chickpea, chickpea flour.

gungá	The Ganges, India's most sacred river. The Goddess of the Ganges.
Gungá Poojáh	Festival in honour of the Ganges.
handy	Earthenware vessel.
Hanumán	Hindu monkey-god, Rama's ally and helper.
hávildár	Indian non-commissioned officer, corresponding in rank to a sergeant.
Huzoor	'The presence'; an exalted way of talking about a superior.
jadu	Magical spell, enchantment.
jemádár	Leader; head servant. Second rank of Indian army officer.
jo hookum	'Your order', meaning 'order received' [from Arabic 'Hukm'].
juloosee	Shining, glittering.
Káli	Hindu destroyer-goddess, an avatar of Devi.
khana	House or compartment. Used to refer to a department.
keráni	Accounts clerk.
khánsámás	House-steward. The chief servant to wait at table.
kincob	Rich Indian fabric embroidered with gold or silver.
kitmutgár	Butler or servant who waits on guests individually at a dinner table.
koorneeshes	Salutation.
koteewál	Police headquarters.
kothee	Cottage.
Krishna	Incarnation of the Hindu god Vishnu. Usually represented as a blue-skinned flute-playing cowherd.
Kshetriya	The second, warrior caste in the Hindu social system.
lakh	One hundred thousand.
lotáh	Water-vessel, usually made of brass.
M'lechha	Polluted untouchable; the lowest caste in the Hindu system of Varna.
Machooá Bazáar	One of the markets of Calcutta.
mahájun	Moneylender, merchant.
maháprasád	Sweets used as a temple offering.

Mahrattá	Marathi-speaking region around present-day Bombay/Mumbai.
mathránis	Female sweeper.
mem	Memsahib: European woman.
mofussil	The countryside; the provinces.
mohurer	Treasury-clerk responsible for counting gold mohurs.
moong-ke-dál	High-quality dal.
moonsiff	Lawyer or legal administrator.
moorgee	Chicken.
moosuk	Watertight leather bags used by water-carriers.
Nabáb	Governor of a region within the Mughal empire [from Persian nawāb].
námamálá	Rosary used by Hindu devotees.
omedwár	Candidate for employment. Literally, 'a hopeful one'.
Ooryáh	Adjective pertaining to the state of Orissa.
páháráwállá	Watchman or gatekeeper.
páik	Foot courier or runner.
pálkee	Palanquin.
pálkee-ghárry	Palanquin-shaped coach.
panchunwálláh	Dealer in all the ingredients for paan.
páwn	Areca-nut wrapped in betel leaf for chewing [from Hindi Paan].
Peishwá	Chancellor. The chief minister of a Mahratta state.
peon	Footman; a pawn in chess [from Portuguese peão].
pice	Small coin, a quarter of an anna.
pilsooj	Lamp-stand.
poddár	Cashier or officer attached to the treasury.
poojáh	Hindu religious ceremony.
puccá	Mature; cooked; well made. Often used to describe housing.
pugree	Cloth wound around a sun-hat.
punka-puller	Servant employed to operate a punkah (ceiling fan).
Rájáh	King; the Hindu head of state.
Rákshasa	Demon in Hindu mythology.

rupee	Currency unit of colonial India.
sabáit	Priest and beneficiary of a temple.
salaám	Blessings (from Arabic).
sepoy	Indian soldier (often used to refer to Indian soldiers in the British army).
shikári	Local hunter or tracker.
shroff	(v. and n.) Clerk employed to sort out good currency from forged or filed coins.
sircár	1) The Government or supreme authority. 2) House steward. 3) Mughal territorial division.
sirdár/surdar	Group leader.
Sontá	Sontha or Santhal. Bengal tribal group originating from south of Bhagalpur.
sowár	Indian cavalry soldier.
subádá kothee	Officer's quarters.
subadár	Officer of a company of Indian soldiers.
syce	Groom.
tálookdárs	Revenue collector; owner of a *taluk* or tract of estate land.
tamáshá	Scene; an entertainment.
Terái	Belt of jungle between the Himalayas and the plains.
Thákoorjee	Honorific reference to a landowner.
thállá	Plate.
ticcá ghárries	Hired coach or trap.
ticcá pálkees	Hired palanquin.
topiwálláh	One who wears European dress; literally, one who wears a solar topi (pith-helmet).
torkáree	Curry.
tullub	To want: an order.
tulwár	Sword. A curved Indian sabre.
Vysnub	Devotee of Vishnu.
zemindár	Landowner.
zenáná	Women's quarters in a Muslim household.